"If there is anything that can combat the violence and hatred consuming our world today, it is forgiveness. Michael Henderson shows this to be true. His remarkable stories demonstrate the power of forgiveness in bringing about world peace—and individual peace as well."

—**Johann Christoph Arnold,** author of *Seventy Times Seven: The Power of Forgiveness*

"With this useful, highly readable book, Michael Henderson makes a meaningful contribution to entering the new millennium in a new spirit."

—**Michael Medved,** film critic and radio host

"Michael Henderson's voice is one of our nation's most powerful and thought-provoking. He offers a counterpoint to the escalation of hostility in our society. Henderson's gentle courage and insight are tools we must all use as we come to grips with a past replete with horror and oppression, and learn to heal history and function as one nation, one world, all the same."

—**Julianne Malveaux,** economist, author, and syndicated columnist

"In a world where the words 'reconciliation' and 'forgiveness' seem little to apply to a world in perpetual rage and conflict, this inspiring book serves to give us hope. These stories of actual human beings and their potential for change and resurrection are themselves transforming."

—**Georgie Anne Geyer,** syndicated columnist, author, and educator

"If anyone has any doubts about the power of forgiveness to heal the hurts of ordinary people and indeed entire nations, he should read Michael Henderson's heart-warming new book."

—**David Aikman,** veteran journalist and author of *Great Souls: Six Who Changed the Century*

"During my diplomatic career, most assignments that came to me were conflict resolution related. As a result I became to believe that we diplomats are remiss in not being able to figure out how to get beyond the cessation of people shooting each other. The 'forgiveness factor' is absolutely essential. Michael Henderson has put together a collection of thoughts and theology which makes it possible for the resolution practitioner to move miles beyond the mere cessation of overt hostility and physical battle."

—**Edward Perkins,** executive director of the International Programs Center, University of Oklahoma, and former U.S. ambassador to Liberia, South Africa and Australia

FORGIVENESS

Also by Michael Henderson
  From India with Hope
  Experiment with Untruth
  A Different Accent
  On History's Coattails
  Hope for a Change
  All Her Paths Are Peace
  The Forgiveness Factor

FORGIVENESS

Breaking the Chain of Hate

Michael Henderson

 BookPartners
Wilsonville, Oregon

Library of Congress Cataloging-in-Publication Data

Henderson, Michael.
    Forgiveness : breaking the chain of hate / Michael Henderson.
       p.   cm.
    Includes bibliographical references and index.
    ISBN 1-581-51050-0 (trade pbk. : alk. paper)
    1. Forgiveness.   I. Title.
    BJ1476.H46   1999
    179'.9 21--dc21   99-40333

Cover design by Richard Ferguson
Text design by Sheryl Mehary

BookPartners, Inc.
P. O. Box 922
Wilsonville, Oregon 97070

Dedicated to Dick and Randy Ruffin
with gratitude for their constant encouragement

Contents

Acknowledgments

I would like to thank those who helped in many different ways, big and small. (If I fail to remember some, I hope that forgiveness is also operative here!):

Jim Baynard-Smith, Dr. K. E. Beazley, Phyllis Bocock, Brian and Juliet Boobbyer, Dale Bowlin, Virginia Brinton, Mika and Jean Brown, Ann Carr, Joe Carter, Cornelia Connelly, Stella Cornelius, Geoffrey Craig, Anthony Duigan, Julia Duin, Will Elliott, Judge Jack Etheridge, Chris Evans, Nico and Loel Ferreira, Maire Fitzpatrick, Rajmohan Gandhi, Rabbi Marc Gopin, Sally Hall, Dr. Bryan Hamlin, Peter and Fiona Hannon, Councillor Mike Hannon, Chris and Ann Hartnell, Peter Hegi, Pieter Horn, Edward Howard, Willard Hunter, Chris Mayor, Joseph Montville, Hugh Nowell, Edward Peters, Sam Pono, Henry Reynolds, Patrick and Barbara Rohde, Bill Stallybrass, George Vondermuhll, Jr., Lawson and Mary Wood.

For permission to reprint copyrighted material, thanks are given to the following publishers, papers or authors. Publication details are in the Bibliography.

Terry Anderson for his poem "Out of Prison"; Ave Maria Press for quotations from Father Jenco in *Bound to Forgive;* Coventry *Evening Telegraph* for a letter from Les Dennison; Stephanie Dowrick for an extract from her book *Forgiveness—and Other Acts of Love;* Rev. Nicholas Frayling for material from his book *Pardon and Peace;* W.W. Norton Publishers for extracts from *The Railway Man* by Eric Lomax; Rabbi Marc Gopin for a quotation from a paper delivered at American University; Lewis B. Smedes for six points from *The Art of Forgiving;* Michael Smith for his work in *For a Change;* Michael Thwaites for his poem "For Yarmuk, Elder of the Ulupna Tribe: from *The Honey Man;* Wilhelm Verwoerd for material from *My Winds of Change;* Anitra Rasmussen for her speech in the Oregon Legislature; Philip Yancey for an extract from his book *What's So Amazing About Grace?*

Naturally, none of my correspondents bears any responsibility for the finished product, but I would particularly acknowledge the help given on chapter 3 by John Bond; chapter 4 by Wilhelm

Verwoerd; chapter 5 by Rev. Nicholas Frayling and Gerald Henderson; chapter 6 by Rev. Paige Chargois and Rob Corcoran; chapter 7 by Olgierd and Aniela Stepan, Tianethone and Viengxay Chantharasy; David Howell, Chris Keeble, Mammo Wudneh, Jack Estes and Colleen O'Callaghan; chapter 8 by Richard Channer, Les Dinnison and John Nunneley; chapter 9 by Dr. Yusuf al-Azhari and Leif Hovelsen; chapter 10 by Denise Wood, Suresh and Lena Khatri, Ratu Meli Vesikula, and Sir Conrad Hunte; chapter 11 by Rev. Stephen Kingsnorth, Peter Biehl, Phillipe Lasserre, Lou Reymen, and Dalia and Yehezkel Landau.

I am grateful to my publishers, Thorn and Ursula Bacon, for their belief in the importance of the subject at this time in history and their confidence that the stories to which I have access could be a contribution to our living together in this new century. And to my editor, Jane McGary, for helping an Englishman be intelligible to Americans.

Preface

I have on my wall a large Snoopy cartoon. Wielding his tennis racket, the cartoon character is observing sagaciously, "Winning isn't everything."

Then he delivers the punchline, "Until you lose."

It is not unlike the subject of this book.

"Everyone says forgiveness is a lovely idea," writes C. S. Lewis. He adds, "Until they have something to forgive."

How often we hear someone running down people in a situation far removed who don't seem to have the sense to get along with one another! The critic implies that we somehow are wiser and better — and more forgiving — than they are. Such smugness about conflict disappears quickly, however, when our will is suddenly crossed, our ambitions thwarted, or our own people denigrated.

So the first thing to be said is that if to forgive may be divine, it is also devilish difficult.

The men and women who have found the strength to forgive deserve our respect; those who are not yet prepared to go that far need our understanding. My hope in writing this book is that those who hesitate may be encouraged by the examples of forgiveness in its stories, and that others may take fresh heart about the world when they set these stories against the daily headlines reflecting violence and vengeance. I sometimes suggest a link between personal and international forgiveness, between what individuals decide and the way nations can be affected, but I leave the social policy and foreign policy implications to those who are better qualified to tackle the subject.

I do not bring to this work much hands-on expertise or academic knowledge: rather, a grateful heart for the fact that over fifty years I have had the good fortune to be associated with and exposed to hundreds of people who have been working for reconciliation and change. They are men and women from every part of the world and from different faiths whose basic philosophy has been that if you want to bring about change in the world, the best place to start is with yourself. They say, paraphrasing President Harry Truman, "The blame stops here."

I wrote a book about some of these friends, and it was clear when it was finished that forgiveness was a common element in the experience of many of them — hence the title, *The Forgiveness Factor*. I then found, as I was invited to promote the book, that I was, to my discomfort, being written up as an expert on the subject.

As I spoke and responded to audiences, I did, however, learn a great deal more about the readiness of people to forgive even in the most painful circumstances, most notably in Australia with the Aborigine people. One New York radio host said to me, "Forgiveness is in." There is a certain superficiality to the comment, but it is true that more and more people — perhaps sparked by the advent of the new millennium — have been ready to draw a line or start afresh, and several books on the subject have come out. In a feature headed, "Apologize now! — everyone's doing it," in *Civilization* (April/May 1999), novelist Jane Smiley writes, "Should the arrow of apology hit the moving target of injury, should the expression of regret or the request that one be offered be read as a request for help, then forgiveness itself is always large enough to reduce the injury and renew the soul."

I stand in awe of the courage and generosity of many people who have been ready to forgive in circumstances that are outside the experience of most of us, and I hope that I will not be found wanting should I be placed in a similar situation. I admire deeply much of the writing and scholarship now coming to the fore in the field of forgiveness; some relevant books are listed in the bibliography.

While saluting valiant attempts to define forgiveness and delineate where forgiveness is or is not appropriate, I find myself fascinated by the exceptions: those people who don't know, for instance, that they should wait for repentance on the part of those who have done them wrong before they forgive; those who are not aware that they should not extend forgiveness to a whole country and go ahead and do so anyway.

Not everyone will agree with everything written in this book. Not everyone needs to apologize or repent (at least in this context!). Some see a close connection between their lives and those of their forebears, recognizing the legacy and perhaps the privileged position that is theirs. Some do not. This book is not about political correctness, nor is it a prescription for everyone. It is about conscience — and, for those who think in such terms, the prompting of the spirit.

I am grateful for the many letters I have received giving insights on the subject of forgiveness and sometimes glimpses of events that have not always had much coverage in the press. For instance, a couple who were present in Russia in July 1998 at the reburial of Tsar Nicholas II describe how President Yeltsin "really spoke from his heart, admitted his own personal wrong and spoke movingly of the need to enter the next century in a spirit of repentance and reconciliation."

One of the most moving letters was from a mother whose son, a British soldier, was killed in Northern Ireland. She was not ready to be included in a book about forgiveness, but her compassion and understanding and breadth of view surely confirmed that she was on that road. And it is, indeed, a road on which most of us at some part of our lives, in smaller or larger scale, may walk if we choose. This mother writes humbly that she looked in her son's coffin and told him that she was "sorry that this conflict had been allowed to go on for so long by my parents' generation and my generation and because of that so many young people like him had lost their lives."

She asks, "Can you forgive people who do not see they have done any wrong in killing your loved one? It is a very easy thing to say the Lord's Prayer but far more difficult to do in real life and I often wonder how many people who say those words about forgiveness have ever had to do it in real life about something so serious."

As I write these words. the agony in the Balkans continues and the settlement in Northern Ireland is limping along. These two areas reflect the hold that historic grievances still have on populations.

As I write, too, we hear of Christians apologizing in Jerusalem on the 900th anniversary of the sacking of the city during the Crusades. Their apologies came at the end of a Reconciliation Walk from Cologne, where the Crusades began, that brought 500

Christians from Europe, Australia and the United States to the Middle East. They came not to evangelize but to ask forgiveness for what was done in the name of Christ and to try to defuse the bitter legacy of the Crusades. One was Prince Albrecht zu Castell-Castell, a descendant of a knight who had killed Muslims and Jews, who apologized to descendants of the Muslim warrior Saladin for his ancestor's crimes which, he said, had burdened his conscience for years. One London newspaper dismissed the Reconciliation Walk as "a pointless exercise" and "an empty gesture" but the mayor of Tel Aviv told the walkers, "Peace will come to the Middle East through people like you."

Neither forgiveness nor its inverse, repentance, will alone solve the world's problems or bring peace. But without those two elements, it is hard to see how settlements will prevail over time. So stories where that hold of history is being healed are also a feature of this book. They show that forgiveness knows no national boundaries and has the power to break the chain of hatred and revenge handed down from one generation to the next.

Michael Henderson
Portland, Oregon
July, 1999

"When we think of forgiveness, the fear may arise that evil will remain unpunished. It is as if forgiving might mean to give up the right to punish evil. Despite all of this I have to see what evil does to me; it makes me want to react to evil with evil. Then I see everything with dark glasses of evil. It paralyses me and alienates me from life. Forgiving means bidding goodye to evil, in order not to be guided by it any more.

"A process of reconciliation may take some time as the other side has to recognize its faults also. With forgiveness, however, I don't need to wait and waste time. Forgiveness gives me freedom to love now. When we attain this freedom, we realize that those who have done evil are themselves its victims.

"In forgiving we do not lose anything, rather we receive a gift."

— Father Andrija Vrane
Bosnia, 1998

1

Receiving a gift

"Forgiveness is not just some nebulous, vague idea that one can easily dismiss. It has to do with uniting people through practical politics. Without forgiveness there is no future."

— Archbishop Desmond Tutu

Alice Wedega was the first woman member of the Papua New Guinea legislature and the first woman in her country to be decorated by the queen of England. At a dinner welcoming Queen Elizabeth to Papua New Guinea in 1973, one of her security guards heard that Alice had visited Northern Ireland. "What on earth were you doing there?" he asked.

In her direct fashion, Alice told the man that her great-grand-father had been a cannibal. "At that time," she said, "our people used to kill and eat men. They would practice payback. That is, if one of your side killed one of mine, my side would kill one of yours. But the missionaries came from Europe to stop us doing all that. And now I have been back to Northern Ireland to help the Europeans there to stop doing it."

Payback.

It would be hard to find a more succinct summation of the problem faced by many individuals and countries round the world. Call it tit-for-tat, revenge, vendetta, or vengeance, the cycle of blame blights lives and generations. It knows no end because practically everyone has something for which they can blame others. This cycle can be broken only by forgiveness, which Lewis B. Smedes has defined as "surrendering the right to get even."

Smedes writes, "Vengeance is a passion to get even. It is a hot desire to give back as much pain as someone gave you. The problem with revenge is that it never gets what it wants; it never evens the score. Fairness never comes. The chain reaction set off by every act of vengeance always takes its unhindered course. It ties both the injured and the injurer to an escalator of pain. Both are stuck on the escalator as long as parity is demanded, and the escalator never stops, never lets anyone off."

The *New Collegiate Dictionary* defines forgiveness as follows: "1) Willingness to cease to feel resentment against an offender; 2) Willingness to grant relief from a payment of debt; 3) Willingness to allow room for error or weakness." *Roget's Thesaurus* gives many words associated with the concept: pardon, exoneration, absolution, dispensation, acquittal, reprieve, amnesty, mercy, forbearance, grace, exculpation, deliverance, indulgence, clemency, compassion, charity. Billy Graham describes forgiveness as "the most glorious word in the English language." Even the cynic Oscar Wilde could advise, "Always forgive your enemies: nothing annoys them so much."

Forgiveness is possibly the most remarkable quality to which the human species can aspire. "The power to forgive," writes Donald Shriver, "remains one of the awesome powers of human being as well as divine being." Writer Peggy Noonan says, "To forgive is to change the world." That is, indeed, what many of the people whose stories are told in this book, on a small and sometimes on a surprisingly large scale, are doing.

Some people may reject the concept of forgiveness without knowing what it is they are rejecting. Smedes, in his book, *The Art of Forgiving,* gives six simple statements of what forgiveness is _not_ about:

1. Forgiving someone who did us wrong does not mean that we tolerate the wrong he did.
2. Forgiving does not mean that we want to forget what happened.
3. Forgiveness does not mean that we excuse the person who did it.
4. Forgiving does not mean that we take the edge off the evil of what was done to us.
5. Forgiving does not mean that we surrender our right to justice.
6. Forgiving does not mean that we invite someone who hurt us once to hurt us again.

Some people, particularly those who approach the subject from a theological or psychological perspective, may be very precise in their definitions. This becomes essential when forgiveness is studied, as it is increasingly, for the part it may play in public policy.

Kenneth Kaunda, former president of Zambia, warns, "To claim forgiveness whilst perpetuating injustice is to live a fiction; to fight for justice without also being prepared to offer forgiveness is to render your struggle null and void." The public and foreign policy establishments have been nervous about forgiveness, particularly when it looks like intruding on their domain. For a long time, the role of forgiveness was outside the considerations of hard-nosed practitioners of Realpolitik and felt to be irrelevant to their work. But recently some excellent books have looked at the wider role forgiveness should be playing.

Donald Shriver, author of *An Ethic for Enemies — Forgiveness in Politics,* writes:

> Slowly, I have arrived at the belief that the concept of forgiveness, so customarily relegated to the realms of religion and personal ethics, belongs to the heart of

reflection about how groups of humans can move to repair the damages that they have suffered from their past conflicts with each other. Precisely because it attends at once to moral truth, history and the human benefits that flow from the conquest of enmity, forgiveness is a word for a multi-dimensional process that is eminently political.

He says that the leftover debris of national pasts that continues to clog the relationships of diverse groups of humans around the world will never get cleaned up and animosity will never drain away "until forgiveness enters those relationships in some political form."

Forgiveness in politics, as in personal life, Brian Frost reminds us, must continue to be understood as a process "rather than something to be applied temporarily, like a poultice."

The idea of forgiveness and the need to surrender the desire for revenge are universal. The Chinese have a saying, "He who opts for revenge must first dig two graves." There is an African proverb: "He who forgives ends the quarrel." A Shawnee chant goes, "Do not wrong or hate your neighbor; for it is not he that you wrong; you wrong yourself."

Fortunately, forgiveness is one of the few concepts which, like love, are respected and encouraged by most of the world's religions. "Learning to forgive someone who has hurt you may be one of life's most demanding, yet most meaningful, tasks," writes Huston Smith in *The World's Religions.* "Forgiveness asks you to reappraise the hurt and its source and to go through a shift in how you think and feel about both the offender and yourself. As a goal commonly advocated by all of the world's long-standing religions, forgiveness can be a truly transforming experience that allows us to move beyond our often selfish desires and needs."

The Dalai Lama, spiritual and political leader of the people of Tibet, has set an example of applying the forgiveness inherent in Buddhism in his relation to the Chinese people, despite the persecution of his people and his own exile. He likes to tell the story of one of his senior monks who spent many years in a Chinese labor camp. When finally given permission to visit India, he came to see the Dalai Lama. His Holiness asked the monk whether he faced many dangers in Tibet. "Yes," he replied, "sometimes there was the danger of losing compassion for the Chinese."

The Dalai Lama suggests that you can learn more from your enemies than from your teachers. Tolerance and forgiveness, he says, are the key methods of minimizing hatred, and you can learn these things from your enemy. You cannot feel hatred, disrespect, or anger toward your guru, and so you cannot learn tolerance, forgiveness, and patience from him, or from your best friend. Hatred usually arises from your enemy. When you meet him, that is the golden opportunity to test how much you practice what you believe. "Our enemy is our ultimate teacher," he says.

Yusuf Omar al-Azhari (whose story appears in chapter 9), is a former Somali ambassador to the United States. He sees forgiveness as the one means that can bring people together, and as a Muslim he has been practicing it in his devastated country, even to the extent of forgiving the dictator who put him in solitary confinement for six years. "In the Islamic religion," he says, "forgiveness is a prerequisite factor to settle any disagreements or disputes or antagonisms that may occcur between people. In the Holy Koran it is often quoted and commends every Muslim to forgive and ask forgiveness regardless of whether one is right or wrong. The Koran stipulates that anyone who forgives or asks forgiveness shall be rewarded by the Almighty, Allah. Therefore it is a must in the Islamic religion that one forgives for wrongs done to him and asks forgiveness for wrongs he inflicted on others."

Rajmohan Gandhi, a grandson of the Mahatma who as much as any Hindu in India has reached out to the Muslim population and to Pakistan, says that the Sanskrit word for forgiveness, *kshama*, occurs in the earliest Hindu texts, including the 1,200-year-old epic, the *Mahabharata*, and in the *Bhagavad-Gita,* the scriptural text to which Hindus turn most. In the *Mahabharata*, he says, though forgiveness is strongly extolled, it is rejected by the epic's characters, and the chain of revenge finally takes almost every life. While not showing the triumph of forgiveness, it demonstrates the futility of revenge. "All in all, forgiveness is not the dominant note in Hindu theology or tradition, but it is recognized as an important and difficult virtue."

Gandhi credits an experience in the area of apology and forgiveness in his own life as the motivator of much of his work for Hindu-Muslim and India-Pakistan reconciliation. In 1951, as a young student, he was in the office of the *Hindustan Times,* of which his father was editor, when a subeditor came in with the news that Liaqat Ali Khan, the prime minister of Pakistan, had been shot. The young Gandhi said to the subeditor, "I hope what follows is news of his death."

Gandhi writes in his book *Eight Lives,* "Liaqat Ali Khan had done me or mine no harm. Our paths had never crossed. But he was Pakistan's prime minister and Pakistan was India's enemy. Moreover, making a heartless remark put a sixteen-year-old in the category of real men, didn't it? And in the category of smart men. But the subeditor did not smile. Not smiling, he made me feel small. The vanity and ill-will that masqueraded in my heart as manliness stood exposed. *Main sharmindu boon* (I am ashamed. And always will be)."

That experience of an exposed pettiness, says Gandhi, made him want to make amends and was a factor in his wishing to write *Eight Lives,* portraits of Muslim leaders in the subcontinent. "More than that, the episode and what it disclosed helped create a longing to heal the subcontinent's wounds." He says that the fact that *Eight Lives* seems to have touched many — Hindus as well as Muslims — was perhaps "because I was willing to face my own heart and to let it be filled with a desire to build bridges."

Rabbi Marc Gopin, who teaches religion and conflict resolution at George Mason University, in a paper presented at American University (February 1999), said that forgiveness had to be a critical adjunct to rational negotiations and justice seeking, because in virtually every long-standing conflict that he had ever seen, from family quarrels all the way to genocide, there was never complete justice — no way to recover the lost lives and the lost time, or to heal the emotional scars of torture and murder. And there was rarely the possibility of achieving everything each group envisioned at the height of struggle and battle. He said:

Thus, in the context of mourning what can not be restored, forgiveness and the creation of new bonds with those who one fought is a vital form of comfort for irrecoverable losses. It offers the possibility of a new matrix, a new cognitive and emotive structure of reality that can not replace the losses but does create a surprisingly new reason to live nonviolently and believe that such a life can be worth living. People recovering from genocide and guilty over their survival, people who have been forfeiting their sons' lives for generations, often need a jolt, an unexpected reason that they may be able to live normally, a reason to believe that a new way of life is not only possible but will actually be better than continuing to mourn their losses and punish those who inflicted those losses. Forgiveness processes can be the soul that animates this new vision of reality in the heart of those who have suffered for so long.

For Frank Buchman, a Christian minister from Pennsylvania, an experience of forgiveness was central to his life's work. He was the initiator of Moral Re-Armament and a source of inspiration to the founders of Alcoholics Anonymous. His work for world peace, through Mountain House, the center of reconciliation in Caux, Switzerland, led to nominations for the Nobel Peace Prize. He traced his effectiveness back to the moment when he asked forgiveness of a board of six directors whom he hated. He had felt that they had treated him wrongly but that he had to ask their forgiveness for the way he had behaved. "I was the seventh wrong man," he often said.

Buchman saw the process of repentance, apology, and asking for and accepting forgiveness as having universal application. After this experience in his own life when he realized his own sin and experienced Christ's forgiveness, he never again, according to his biographer Garth Lean, "considered that any other human being, however corrupted, was beyond the reach of the grace which had healed his own hate and pride."

In 1978 Matt Manson, a Scotsman working in Asia, heard an unexpected story about forgiveness on a flight from Melbourne to Hong Kong. It had a powerful effect on his life. Given seat F13, he found to his surprise that the occupant of seat F14 was the Nobel peace laureate, Mother Teresa of Calcutta, who after her death in 1999 was placed in candidacy for sainthood.

Over the course of the nine-hour flight Matt Manson and Mother Teresa talked about a number of things. At one point she said to the Scotsman, "Forgiveness is the greatest thing in the world." Their work as Sisters of Charity, she told him, was to mediate forgiveness, for without it there was no reconciliation between God and man, or man and man. It was the key to the survival of mankind: "This is what I want to see in the lives of all who come and serve with me. Our work is not just to bind the wounds and care in a social way for the dying. Our work is to mediate an experience of forgiveness to those whom we are caring for."

She illustrated this by a story. She and some of her nuns were working in the alleyways of Calcutta, finding those who needed care and putting them into an ambulance to transport them back to the House for the Dying. She was about to close the door of the ambulance when she heard the cry of an old woman. She looked out and along the street and could see no one. But the cry persisted. Then she spotted a trash can against the wall. Looking in, she found an old woman, bleeding and in a terrible state. "Please, please help me," said the old woman. "My son put me here to die."

"So we got her out and took her with the rest back to the House. We washed her, prepared her and cared for her. That night was one of the most arduous I have ever had in my life: the prayer, the perseverance, the persistence of the sisters to get that old woman to the point where she could forgive her son." It went on all night.

In the early hours of the morning the woman said, "Just a minute, I want to say something to you. I can remember well the day when my son was a young boy and something happened. I shut him out of my home and closed my heart to him. It has never been opened since. From that point that boy took the wrong path. I am to blame because he had no one to turn to."

Mother Teresa said to her, "If we got him here now would you ask him to forgive you?"

She replied, "Yes, yes, find him. Find him." And she told the sisters where to go. They moved out fast and found the son, a man in very great need and trouble. They persuaded him to come with them. Mother and son confronted each other.

"It was a moment of anguish," Mother Teresa told her flight companion. "We did not know what would happen."

The mother said to the son, "Son, I shut you out of my life when you were a boy. You had nobody to turn to. I am to blame for the life of misery that you have to lead. Will you please forgive me?"

Then the man — a tough man — suddenly broke down and wept. "Of course, of course," he said. "But will you forgive me?"

Shortly afterward, the woman died. "But she was serene, she was at peace," said Mother Teresa. "She had found a reconciliation not only with her son but with God."

Mother Teresa had with her a sack of letters, her only baggage. These letters, she explained, were from young women from all over India and many parts of the world offering to come, to give everything they had, accepting the vows of poverty, chastity and obedience, ready to live in any part of the world where the need was great. "Between now and Calcutta," said the nun, "I have to answer these letters and make sure that each one of these people who have written to me is able to mediate the experience we mediated to that woman. You can't do that unless you yourself have faced fully your sin and let Jesus deal with it. If you have experienced forgiveness in your own life, you will be equipped. I want to make sure that each one of those who have written to me has had that experience before moving into this work. If they don't have that, they may be with us for five years, maybe even ten years. But sooner or later if that is not a reality they will die on the vine."

Matt Manson said later, "As I left the plane at Hong Kong, I reflected on all she had told me. It meant a rededication of my life to serve and be an instrument to mediate forgiveness."

It is difficult to conceive of forgiveness operating in the midst of armed hostilities, or in the midst of a liberation struggle, although a forgiving spirit can still prevail over taking pleasure in the suffering of others. Smedes reports a conversation with a black leader in South Africa at a time when Nelson Mandela was still in prison and people could only hope against hope for change. The man said to him, "Ah, yes, forgiveness, it will have to come to that sometime, but not yet, not while the boot is still on our neck." Similarly, Dietrich Bonhoeffer, who was murdered by the Nazis, concluded in his *Letters and Papers from Prison* that forgiveness would have to come, but not until "violence has become justice, lawlessness become order and war has become peace."

Some people are not prepared to forgive until some formal evidence of closure exists. Myrlie Evers-Williams, former chair of the NAACP, is one example. Her husband, a civil rights leader, was murdered in Mississippi. For many years, as she writes in her auto-biography *Watch Me Fly,* she was "raging, brimming over with deep, dark loathing and despair," secretly imagining her revenge, torturing whoever was responsible for her huband's death. It was only when her husband's killer was finally brought to justice that healing was possible for her soul and for the soul of Mississippi. "Hatred was released, the hatred I had thought was gone, but that always managed to creep back in." Likewise, the Irish nationalist P. J. McClean, who was tortured by British forces when he was a prisoner in the Long Kesh camp in Northern Ireland, realized that his hatred was not going to answer the violence and injustice in his homeland; but he believes that he was able to get rid of that "baggage of bitterness and grievance" only because he won redress from the British government for his mistreatment.

Yet, when all is said and done, forgiveness remains a mystery and cannot be confined by theory. It is hard to discover why some people will forgive and others will not. From the chapters that follow, spanning a wide variety of experience, readers may form their own conclusions.

2

Healing history: A new technology for the 21st century?

"History, despite its wrenching pain
Cannot be unlived, but if faced with courage
Need not be lived again."

— Maya Angelou

In a debate in Britain's House of Commons, Winston Churchill once referred to then Prime Minister Stanley Baldwin with the words, "History will say that the right honorable gentleman was wrong in this matter." Then, after a pause, he added, "I know it will, because I shall write the history."

There will always be quarrels about how to interpret the past. Historic figures will, like fashions, come into favor or be relegated by academics to obloquy or obscurity. Even Churchill now faces an occasional uncomfortable reassessment. In the past, the interpretations of history, though irritating, perhaps mattered less; but as the world shrinks and at the same time splinters, a more balanced history, and an understanding of the forces that have shaped attitudes, is becoming crucial. Moreover, some peoples who have rarely had the luxury of writing histories, like Native Americans and African-Americans, are now telling their stories. As Caryl Phillips, a British writer of West Indian heritage, puts it, "If history is an interview with the winners, I'm interested in the losers."

Oradour, Ravensbruck, Jallianwallabagh, Bloody Sunday, the Battle of the Boyne, Pearl Harbor, Guernica, Wounded Knee, Auschwitz, My Lai, Katyn, Sharpeville, Dresden: these names may not be familiar to everyone, but in many whose history is involved, their very utterance evokes an emotional response. These and dozens of other such names from every continent are shorthand for historic scars that need care and healing.

Can history be healed?

In 1847, when the United States was at war with Mexico, a decisive battle was fought at Chapultepec, a castle on the outskirts of Mexico City. The defenders were military cadets who decided to die rather than surrender; they became known to Mexicans as the "Boy Heroes of Chapultepec." It became Mexico's Alamo. At the close of the war the following year, by the terms of the Treaty of Guadalupe Hidalgo, Mexico ceded to the United States two-fifths of its territory — including Texas, California, Arizona, New Mexico, Nevada, Utah, and part of Colorado. In return, the U.S. paid Mexico $15 million in indemnity and assumed $3 million more in claims against Mexico. The Mexican war was one of the reasons why the U.S. has been resented in Latin America for two centuries.

On the hundredth anniversary of the Battle of Chapultepec, and without great fanfare, President Harry Truman visited Mexico and made a gesture of healing. He visited Chapultepec Castle and laid a wreath on the tomb of the "Boy Heroes." It was the first time a U.S. leader had publicly acknowledged this source of national pain. One headline read, "Truman heals an old national wound forever." Truman's biographer, David McCullough, wrote that by this courtesy the president "did more to improve Mexican-American relations than had any president in a century."

One man who has made it his priority to study what is needed in healing historical feuds is Joseph Montville, a former State

Department officer who runs the preventive diplomacy program at the Center for Strategic and International Studies in Washington, D.C. He maintains that traditional concepts of peacemaking and diplomacy rarely take into account the psychological influence on individuals, groups, and nations of traumatic or violent attack and grievous loss. "Many of our less successful peace agreements," he maintains, "are so because there has been no underlying process of healing relationships. To me this is a new technology for the twenty-first century."

Montville has been trying over a number of years to help his former colleagues see what role unofficial diplomacy might have in such situations. In 1980, in an article in *Foreign Policy,* Montville described such unofficial initiatives as "Track Two diplomacy," in contrast with the more formal official methods of "Track One diplomacy." This is being increasingly accepted as part of integrated strategies for resolving conflict.

Montville is particularly focusing on the question of ethnic and sectarian conflict, which usually involves people who have endured aggression and loss simply because they are part of an identifiable group, not because of anything they have done. They may have had a sense of fairness until they suffered aggression and loss. Now they distrust the authors of their loss or their descendants in any negotiation or interaction. They may feel they have lost control over their lives and are vulnerable to new attack. "The aggressors or their descendants have never acknowledged that the original act or acts of aggression were unjust," says Montville. "The aggressors or their descendants have not expressed regret or remorse for their acts. They have never genuinely apologized or asked forgiveness of the victim group for their aggression."

Montville suggests that what is needed in that context is an "acknowledgment–contrition–forgiveness transaction." He says the interactive part of the healing begins when the aggressors or their successors acknowledge the tragedy and injustice of recent or historic losses. This tells the victim group that the aggressors or their successors recognize that the aggression was unjust and the victims group's losses were terrible and unjustifiable violations of their basic human rights — even if the aggressors do not explicitly use such words. "When the acknowledgment is sincere, complete and detailed, the victim group can begin to believe that it is possible to trust the good faith of the aggressors in current negotiations and future relationships."

Explicit and sincere expressions of remorse or contrition by the aggressors, he believes, can have a profound healing effect on the victim group. If such expressions are accompanied by a formal apology and request for forgiveness, the healing process will be under way. The fact that this may not immediately produce an explicit grant of forgiveness does not mean that the act has not had an effect. "The challenge of peace," he says, "may take time for testing before it begins to feel safe emotionally. Nevertheless, if a dialogue process can produce a sincere acknowledgment — contrition — forgiveness transaction, then a healing process in the political and human relationship of two peoples will have been launched and will be reflected in concrete, practical ways."

Montville, who has been called in to assist in places as varied as the Middle East, the former Yugoslavia, and Northern Ireland, practices his own philosophy in his approach to the Jewish community. In the course of a speech to the American Psychoanalytic Association in New York, he described Israelis fearing a mass of hostile Arabs surrounding them and waiting for the right moment to push them into the sea, and, in what he called "a doubly wrenching twist of cruel fate," their fear that the gentile world would watch passively, while feigning shocked outrage, as the Arabs completed the "final solution" to the "Jewish problem."

Speaking as a Christian, Montville outlined the terrible things done over centuries to Jews in the name of Christ, creating what he called "the most painful and perhaps the most dangerous of historic grievances, that is of Jews against gentiles, against Christians." "I want to take advantage of this public occasion," he said, "to ask as a private, individual Christian, the forgiveness of the Jewish people for the hurts inflicted on them by Christendom. I ask to be permitted to mourn Jewish losses with Jews and then work in brotherly alliance with Jews and Arabs to mourn unjust hurts suffered by some Arabs as Jews fleeing Christian brutality in Europe established a homeland in Palestine and ultimately the state of Israel. And I want to work with Jews and Arabs to establish a relationship which assures a secure and just future for them and their children."

Another writer who has explored the role of historic enmities in influencing current conflicts is Michael Ignatieff. In *The Warrior's Honor,* he says that the chief moral obstacle in the path of reconciliation is the desire for revenge, and that its deeply moral hold on people is rarely understood. Looked at from the moral point of view, revenge is a desire to keep faith with the dead — to honor their memory by taking up the cause where they left off. Reconciliation is difficult precisely because it must compete with the powerful alternative morality of violence: "Reconciliation means breaking the spiral of intergenerational vengeance. It means substituting the vicious downward spiral of violence with the virtuous upward spiral of mutually reinforcing respect. Reconciliation can stop the cycle of vengeance only if it can equal vengeance as a form of respect for the dead." He goes on, "Without an apology, without recognition of what happened, the past cannot return to its place as the past."

As the world nears the end of the second millennium, it is striking to notice how many countries and individuals seem to be ready to face up to past abuses. Referring to a "veritable avalanche of apologies," Deborah Tannen, professor of Linguistics at Georgetown University, writes, "We humans need apologies to make it possible to continue living in groups. This has always been true in private relationships, and it is true to an ever-increasing degree in public life."

Take the year 1998 as an example. Some may have seen it as the year of hurricane Mitch, and others the year of Monica: disasters natural and unnatural. Yet it was in many ways the year of Mandela-like attitudes and actions: people who rose above the unfair hands dealt them, and nations that were trying to draw a line under past abuses and exploitations. They were not always getting it right but nevertheless trying — not forgetting, but forgiving. A partial list is revealing:

Legislatures, churches, organizations in Australia apologized to the Aborigine people for the way their children were taken from them and often abused.

The United Church of Canada similarly apologized to Native Americans for their abuse at church-operated schools.

The Prime Minister of Japan apologized to British ex-prisoners of war for his country's treatment of them.

The Italian president apologized to the people of Ethiopia for the occupation of their country.

The Pope apologized to Jews for the shortcomings of the church in confronting Nazism in World War II.

The Good Friday agreement was signed in Northern Ireland, with the Nobel Peace Prize being awarded to a Catholic and a Protestant political leader, and an interim peace accord was established in the Middle East.

The report of the Truth and Reconciliation Commission in South Africa was released.

The British prime minister apologized to the Irish for Britain's role in the famine 150 years earlier, reopened the enquiry into Bloody Sunday, and spoke to the Irish Parliament.

President Clinton apologized in Africa for the slave trade.

The President of Argentina apologized to the British for the Falklands/Malvinas War.

In October of that year, Ecuador and Peru ended one of Latin America's longest territorial disputes, which had sparked three wars and caused hundreds of deaths. Ecuadorian President Jamil Mahuad declared, "After so many decades during which both sides tried to win the war, today our two countries will together win the peace." Peruvian President Alberto Fujimori said similarly, "Both countries are winners because both have achieved peace."

The same month saw the start of a new partnership between Japan and South Korea. Japanese Prime Minister Keizo Obuchi, referring to his country's 35-year colonial rule of Korea, said, "This joint declaration will be a new start. I feel acute remorse and offer an apology from my heart." South Korean Prime Minister Kim Dae-jung said, "We must settle the accounts of the twentieth century as we enter the twenty-first century."

It is an impressive list of actions in one year. Some were seen as not going far enough, some as going too far. Some of the agreements may not hold. But the fact that the attempts were made should be honored. Perhaps even more impressive than these apologies has been the willingness of those at the receiving end of abuse to forgive. The year 1998 could have been termed the "Year of Loving Dangerously."

The person who has perhaps most tried to direct the attention of the world to the importance of penitence and forgiveness in the healing of history is Pope John Paul II. One of the Pope's proposals was for an "examination of the conscience at the end of the Millennium." He felt that this reexamination was necessary for the proclamation of the Gospel to the men and women of the third millennium. It was also demanded out of a sense of loyalty and truth in confronting oneself, one's own experience, one's own conscience. This conviction was first reported in *La Stampa* in November 1993: "At the end of the second millennium we must make an examination of conscience: where we are, where Christ has brought us, where we have deviated from the Gospel."

John Paul's proposal was spelled out more fully in a papal memorandum to the cardinals the following spring, entitled "Reflections on the great jubilee of the year two thousand." After recalling the church's recent revocation of its condemnation of the astronomer Galileo, "to remedy the injustice inflicted on him," he goes on in the final paragraph, headed *Reconciliatio et Paenitentia* ("Reconciliation and Penitence"):

A close look at the history of the second millennium can perhaps provide evidence of other similar errors, or even faults, as regards respect for the autonomy due the sciences. How can we be silent about so many kinds of violence perpetrated in the name of the faith? Religious wars, courts of the Inquisition, and other violations of the rights of the human person. In the light of what Vatican II has said, the Church must on its own initiative examine the dark places of its history and judge it in the light of Gospel principles. It could be a grace of the coming Great Jubilee. It would not in any way damage the moral prestige of the Church; on the contrary, it would be strengthened by the manifestation of loyalty and courage in admitting the errors committed by its members and, in a certain sense, in the name of the Church.

In *When a Pope Asks Forgiveness,* author Luigi Accattoli has collected ninety-four quotations in which the pontiff admits the past failures of the church or asks pardon for them. They range from the Inquisition and the Crusades to the Holocaust and the treatment of blacks. In twenty-five of these excerpts he uses the expression "I ask forgiveness" or its equivalent. Some of these statements have had wide press coverage, but most have passed unnoticed. "The Pope," Accattoli writes, "wants to lead the Church into the Third Millennium less burdened by the weight of history, better reconciled with the other Christian communities, and with a bond of friendship with every religion. And if that should cause some degree of confrontation with history, it will not be the end of the world."

In October 1992, for instance, in a message to the indigenous peoples of the Americas, John Paul wrote, "As Pastor of the Church, I ask you in the name of Jesus Christ, to pardon those who have caused pain to you and your ancestors during these 500 years." In May 1995, during a visit to the Czech Republic, the Holy Father referred to the religious wars and said, "Today, in the name of all Catholics, and as Pope of the Church of Rome, I ask forgiveness for the injustices inflicted on non-Catholics in the course of the troubled history of these peoples."

John Paul has also strongly addressed issues of war and peace. Indeed, Accattoli believes that no other pope has preached on peace with the energy of the present one — at least none in the modern age. "And no Pope has ever confessed the sin of war committed by Christians and asked for forgiveness as he has done."

Pope John Paul considers World War II to be the most atrocious scandal in history because it was waged on a continent permeated with Christian traditions. In an Apostolic Letter marking the fiftieth anniversary of the outbreak of that war, he wrote, "We have just recalled one of the bloodiest wars in history, a war which broke out on a continent with a Christian tradition. Acknowledgment of this fact compels us to make an examination of conscience about the quality of Europe's evangelization. The collapse of Christian values that led to yesterday's moral failures must make us vigilant as to the way the Gospel is proclaimed and lived out today."

The Pope has met with the native people of the Americas and every other continent more than forty times, five times acknowledging the historical injustices done to them by Christians. In October 1992, returning from meeting with Native Americans in Phoenix and in Santo Domingo, he spoke about his "act of atonement." He said, "We do not cease asking these people for 'forgiveness.' This request for pardon is primarily addressed to the first inhabitants of the new land, the Indians, and then to those who were brought from Africa as slaves to do heavy labor. 'Forgive us our trespasses.'"

Pope John Paul uttered his strongest words against the sinful treatment of blacks when he visited the house of slaves on the island of Gorée in Senegal in February 1992. He stated that the treatment of Africans was a "tragedy of the civilization that claimed to be Christian" and compared it with extermination camps in Germany. In a meeting with the Catholic community there, he said:

> The visit to the 'slave house' recalls to mind that enslavement of black people which in 1462 Pius II, writing to a missionary bishop who was leaving for Guinea, described as the 'enormous crime,' the *magnum scelus*. Throughout a whole period of the history of the African continent, black men, women and children were brought to this cramped space, uprooted from their land and separated from their loved ones to be sold as goods. They came from all different countries and, parting in

chains for new lands, they retained as their last image of their native Africa Gorée's basalt rock cliffs. We could say that this island is fixed in the memory and heart of all the black diaspora.

These men, women and children were the victims of a disgraceful trade in which people who were baptized, but did not live their faith, took part. How can we forget the enormous suffering inflicted, the violation of the most basic human rights, on those people deported from the African continent? How can we forget the human lives destroyed by slavery?

In all truth and humility this sin of man against man, this sin of man against God, must be confessed. How far the human family still has to go until its members learn to look at and respect one another as God's image, in order to love one another as sons and daughters of their common heavenly Father!

From this African shrine of sorrow, we implore heaven's forgiveness. We pray that in the future Christ's disciples will be totally faithful to the observation of the commandment of fraternal love which the Master left us. We pray that never again will people oppress their brothers and sisters, whoever they may be, but always seek to imitate the compassion of the Good Samaritan in the Gospel in going to help those who are in need. We pray that the scourge of slavery and all its effects may disappear forever. Do not recent tragic events on this continent too invite us to be watchful and continue this lengthy, laborious process of conversion of heart?

The Pope's principal message to Islam can be summed up as follows: Christian and Muslims are brothers under God; they should strive to rise above the past wars that have separated them; and they can do this only by mutual forgiveness. He has several times used the word "brother," which no previous pope has used in addressing Muslims — among other places, in his invitations to Muslims to join him for prayer at Assisi in 1986 and 1993. At Assisi in 1993 he prayed, "For all those who acknowledge Abraham as their father in faith: Jews, Christians, Muslims; that every lack of understanding and every obstacle may be removed and they may all collaborate to work for peace."

In February of the previous year John Paul had said, speaking in northern Nigeria at Kaduna: "All of us, Christians and Muslims, live under the sun of the one merciful God. We both believe in the one God who is the Creator of man. We acclaim God's sovereignty and we defend man's dignity as God's servant. We adore God and profess total submission to him. Thus, in a true sense, we can call one another brothers and sisters in faith in the one God."

He has used the words "courage to forgive" in reference to Islamic extremists. Even two days after the May 1996 murder of seven Trappist monks in Algeria, he said in his Sunday message: "Despite our deep sorrow, we thank God for the witness of love given by those religious. Their fidelity and constancy honor the Church and they will certainly be a seed of reconciliation and peace for the Algerian people, with whom they were in solidarity. May our prayer also reach their families, the Cistercian Order and the small ecclesiastical community in Algeria: in this tragic trial may they never lack the courage of forgiveness and the strength of hope."

The superior of these monks, perhaps foreseeing what would happen to them, had sent a message to friends and relatives in France three months earlier:

> If they seize me some day to become a victim of the terrorism which seems to threaten all the foreigners who live in Algeria today, I would want my community, my Church and my family to remember that I have given my life to God and to this country.
>
> I have lived long enough to consider myself an accomplice in the evil which, alas!, seems to prevail in the world and also in that which can unexpectedly happen to me. If that moment comes, I would like to have the spark of lucidity that would enable me to ask pardon of God and of my brothers in humanity, and at the same time with all my heart to pardon him who has struck me.

I cannot hope for such a death. It seems important to me to declare it. In fact, I don't see how I could rejoice in the fact that a people I love should indiscriminately be accused of my murder. It would be too high a price to pay for what is called 'the grace of martyrdom' ... I know well the contempt in which the Algerians are held throughout the world. I also understand the caricature of Islam which is fostered by a certain form of Islamism.

It is all too easy to put one's conscience at rest by identifying this religion with the fundamentalism of its extremists. For me, Algeria and Islam are something else; they are a body and a soul.

And you, too, friend of my last moment, who will not have realized what you have done, Yes, to you also I want to say thanks and farewell ... And if it is granted us good thieves to meet again in Paradise, it will be the will of God, our common Father. Amen!

A Cry from Croatia

Pray for that bastard?
No, God can't expect me to do a thing like that!
I love my friends, I love meadows, woods, the sea …
I'll pray for plants and animals,
For when they die, our planet dies.
But to pray for that bastard and other trash?
Isn't that too much to ask?

No, it's too little.
How do you expect to change the world
If your love extends only to those who belong to you,
If your love creates camps:
We on the one side, they on the other,
Friends on one side, enemies on the other.
You have no faith if that's how you divide the world.
You have no faith, though you are baptised,
Though you go to mass on Sunday,
Though you give your old clothes to charity.

You have no faith, as long as you love only your friends.
The world does not change through you,
Everything remains the way it was,
And the earth will slowly die from your love.

Yes, the enemy hinders our growth,
He has robbed you of your heritage,
He has settled on your land.
You can hear him laughing in your home, from which
You have been driven away.

Yes, all this is true.
But you have no faith if you do not pray for him,

If you do not befriend him.

Only love such as this can change the world,
Build cities out of rubble,
Allow water to well up in deserts,
Make life come out of death.

And you will no longer see any enemies on your horizon.
Now you are like a phoenix arising from the ashes of
    your home.
And all will be made new, new, new.

— Ljiljana Matkovic-Vlasic

3

National Sorry Day: Australians face up to their past

"True reconciliation between the Australian nation and its indigenous people is not achievable in the absence of acknowledgment by the nation of the wrongfulness of the past dispossession, oppression and degradation of the Aboriginal peoples. That is not to say that individual Australians who had no part in what was done in the past should feel personal guilt. It is simply to assert that national shame, as well as national pride, can and should exist in relation to past acts and omissions, at least when done or made in the name of the community or with the authority of government. Where there is no room for national pride or national shame about the past, there can be no national soul."

— Sir William Deane, Governor-General of Australia

In many countries, European colonization has brought about the devastation of indigenous culture, particularly where the colonizers became the majority population. Now these countries are struggling to overcome a culture of despair among their indigenous people, often expressed in appalling rates of ill health and addiction. Australians are confronting this issue vigorously.

Britain's colonization of Australia began in 1788, and the story of Australia's Aboriginal peoples for the next 150 years was one of dispossession and massacre, to the point where it was widely assumed that they would die out. But the number of people of mixed Aboriginal and white race grew steadily; and since they were almost always born of white fathers and Aboriginal mothers, most of them grew up in Aboriginal communities.

This alarmed the white authorities, who looked on Aboriginal culture as worthless. In their view, if they denied these children all access to Aboriginal culture, Australia would soon become a wholly Western country. So, from the late 1800s, in many parts of Australia the authorities adopted a practice of removing the children from their Aboriginal parents and placing them with white foster parents or in white institutions.

The practice of child removal went on into the 1970s. Most white Australians who knew of it thought that it was justified by the wretched living conditions of many Aboriginals, and they accepted the argument that the children could thereby receive the benefits of Western society. Little attention, however, was given to improving Aboriginal living standards.

In 1995 "Fiona," an Aboriginal woman, described her experiences in words which could be repeated thousands of times across the country:

> In 1936 it was. I would have been five. We went visiting Ernabella the day the police came. We had been playing all together, just a happy community and the air was filled with screams because the police came and mothers tried to hide their children and blacken their children's faces and tried to hide them in caves. We three, Essie, Brenda and me together with our three cousins, the six of us were put on my old truck and taken to Oodnadatta which was hundreds of miles away and then we got there in the darkness. My mother had to come with us. She had already lost her eldest daughter down to the Children's Hospital because she had polio, and

now there was the prospect of losing her three other children, all the children she had. I remember that she came in the truck with us curled up in the fetal position. Who can understand that, the trauma of knowing that you're going to lose all your children? We talk about it from the point of view of our trauma but our mother, to understand what she went through, I don't think anyone can really understand that. We went to the United Aborigines Mission in Oodnadatta. We got there in the dark and then we didn't see our mother again. She just kind of disappeared into the darkness.

These are the words Fiona gave in evidence before an Australian Royal Commission, describing her abduction from her mother. She was not to see her again until 1968: "When I finally met my mother through an interpreter she said that she had heard about the other children, but because my name had been changed she'd never heard about me."

Some white Australians have worked courageously to overcome the attitudes that allowed such cruelty to happen. One was a member of Parliament, Kim Beazley, whose son is the leader of the Labor Party in the Australian Parliament. He decided to make the needs of the Aboriginal people a priority of his parliamentary career. He realized that if Aboriginals did not own land — and they owned none in the three million square miles of Australia — they would always negotiate from a position of weakness. So he persuaded his party to adopt a policy of Aboriginal land rights. He traveled 21,000 miles around the country interviewing hundreds of Aborigines. He was struck by their grace toward a majority people at whose hands they had endured persecution.

Beazley began a variety of initiatives to treat Aborigines with a dignity befitting their position as the first Australians. When he became minister for education, one of his first acts was to arrange for Aboriginal children to be taught in their own languages in primary school. "To deny a people an education in their own language is to treat them as a conquered people," he said. Schools ceased to be alien places for Aboriginal people. With his colleagues, he also set in motion initiatives that led to Aborigines' owning an area of land larger than Great Britain.

International figures also focused on the needs of Aboriginal Australians. When Pope John Paul II visited Australia in 1986, he said, "Christian people of good will are saddened to realize — many of them only recently — for how long a time Aboriginal people were transported from their homelands into small areas or reserves where families were broken up, tribes split apart, children orphaned and people forced to live like exiles in a foreign country."

Such voices encouraged the Australian authorities to look more searchingly at Aboriginal problems. In the late 1980s, the Labor Government initiated a royal commission to discover why so many Aboriginal people took their own lives in prison. The commission report made various recommendations, but said that the underlying need was to improve relations between Aboriginals and non-Aboriginals by a definite process of encouraging understanding.

The government took up this recommendation by forming the Council for Aboriginal Reconciliation. This council was chaired by a powerful Aboriginal spokesman, Patrick Dodson; the deputy chair was Ian Viner, a former minister in a Conservative government. Under their leadership, programs were arranged around the country where police, public servants, and many others could meet the Aboriginal people of their area in forums which encouraged creative discussion.

Ian Spicer, who as chief executive of the Australian Chamber of Commerce and Industry was asked to serve on the Council for Aboriginal Reconciliation, believes that, despite conflicts, there has been significant progress: "For the first time in our history, every person is forced to face their attitude to Aboriginal Australia. No one can avoid the issues." The problems could not be fixed by money alone. Content and understanding had to be provided. Spicer had found that out through sitting down and talking with Aboriginal people. "It gives a great depth to being a citizen of Australia," he says, "that we have in this country an incredible culture which places such importance on the balance between what the land can provide and what individuals can demand from it. It injects into our Anglo-Saxon culture the importance of viewing the whole of life, not just the economic side of it."

An indication of the growing readiness of some Australians — including some government officials — to admit how cruelly the Aboriginal people had been treated is seen in a 1993 speech by Prime Minister Paul Keating. He told Aboriginals in Sydney:

> It is we who did the dispossessing. We took the traditional way of life. We brought the diseases and alcohol. We committed the murders. We took the children from their mothers. We practised discrimination and exclusion. It was our ignorance and prejudice. With some noble exceptions we failed to make the most basic human response and enter in their hearts and minds. We failed to ask: "How would I feel if this were done to me?" We failed to see what we were doing degraded all of us.

In 1992 the Australian High Court made a momentous decision recognizing traditional indigenous land title in common law. This overthrew the 200-year-old constitutional myth that Australia was an empty land when the whites arrived.

Progress was being made toward creating attitudes of respect between the races. But one issue kept raising its head — the continuing effect of the policies of removing Aboriginal children from their parents. A book by an Aboriginal, Margaret Tucker, *If Everyone Cared,* published in 1977, brought this issue to the attention of the Australian public in a way that forced people to reevaluate the widely held view that the children were taken out of wretched conditions for their own good. She describes her own abduction in graphic terms:

> As we hung onto our mother she said fiercely, "They are my children and they are not going away with you." The policeman, who no doubt was doing his duty, patted his handcuffs, which were in a leather case on his belt and which May and I thought was a revolver. "Mrs. Clements,"

he said, "I'll have to use this if you do not let us take these children now."

Thinking the policeman would shoot mother, because she was trying to stop him, we screamed, "We'll go with him, mum, we'll go." I cannot forget any detail of that moment, it stands out as though it were yesterday. I cannot ever see kittens taken from their mother cat without remembering that scene. It is just on sixty years ago.

But Margaret Tucker's book is also written with a remarkable generosity of spirit. She says:

Color is not the issue, the answer is there for all to see: not who is right but what is right. I make many mistakes and don't always have the courage to right those mistakes, but as long as I live, I pray with God's help, I can fight that old snake of hate and bitterness, when he rears his head. Hate does more harm to the hater than to the hated because it makes you ineffective in dealing with the cause of hatred. Hatred can be cured, I know, because it has happened to me.

The Royal Commission into Aboriginal Deaths in Custody investigated ninety-nine deaths and was startled to discover that forty-three of those people had been separated from their families as children. It became clear that this needed proper investigation. The government set up a "National Inquiry into the Separation of Aboriginal and Torres Strait Islander Children from Their Families," to be conducted by the Human Rights and Equal Opportunity Commission. To take charge of the inquiry, the government chose a former high court judge, Sir Ronald Wilson, a West Australian who flew Spitfires during World War II and then pursued a legal career with distinction. Asssisting him was the Aboriginal and Torres Strait Islander Social Justice Commissioner, Mick Dodson.

The commission of inquiry visited every state and territory capital and most regions of Australia. It took evidence in public and private sittings from indigenous people, government and church representatives, former mission staff, foster and adoptive parents, doctors and health professionals, academics, police, and others. A total of 777 people and organizations provided evidence or submissions; 535 were indigenous people, most of whom had been abducted as children.

Sir Ronald says:

> This inquiry was like no other I have undertaken. Others were intellectual exercises, a matter of collating information and making recommendations. But for these people to reveal what had happened to them took immense courage and every emotional stimulus they could muster. They weren't speaking with their mind; they were speaking from the heart. And my heart had to open if I was to understand it.
>
> At each session, the tape would be turned on and we would wait. I would look into the face of the person who was to speak to us. I would see the muscles straining to hold back the tears. But tears would stream down, still no words being spoken. And then hesitantly, words would come. We sat there as long as it took. We heard the story, told with the person's whole being, reliving experiences which had been buried deep, sometimes for decades. They weren't speaking with their minds, they were speaking with their hearts. And my heart had to open if I was to understand them.
>
> I began to realise that the children had been removed because the Aboriginal race was seen as an embarrassment to white Australia. The aim was to strip the children of their Aboriginality, and accustom them to live in a white Australia. The tragedy was compounded when the children, as they grew up, encountered the racism which shaped the policy, and found themselves rejected by the very society for which they were being prepared.

Sir Ronald had been moderator of the Presbyterian Church in Western Australia at the time his church ran Sister Kate's Home, where "stolen children" grew up. "I was proud of the home, with its system of cottage families. Imagine my pain when I discovered, during this Inquiry, that children were sexually abused in those cottages."

The 680-page report was finished in April 1997 and was titled *Bringing Them Home*. It contained fifty-four recommendations that ranged over compensation and apologies, education, standards for indigenous children in state care, the juvenile justice system, counseling services and research. It called for a national apology.

By now, however, a new government had come to power, and their view was that Aboriginal people had been given too much, and the time had come to "swing the pendulum back." They found the report a major embarrassment and tried to bury it.

But national attitudes were changing. The Council for Aboriginal Reconciliation by now had been at work for six years. Thanks to its encouragement, hundreds of study circles had been established, bringing Aboriginal and non-Aboriginal people together all over the country. In May 1997 it held a major convention in Melbourne. It was attended by 1,800 people and had been preceded by 100 regional meetings involving 12,000 people around Australia. At this convention, Sir Ronald presented *Bringing Them Home* to the nation.

The report shook the conscience of Australia. It sold far more than any comparable report, and a shortened version was also prepared; the two together sold more than 70,000 copies. According to Alan Thornhill, the Associated Press correspondent in Canberra, it was the biggest news story of the year. Australians had believed that Aborigines had been taken out of wretched conditions to be offered the benefits of white society — and, indeed, some had been cared for well and altruistically. But the report revealed that many were not: there had been widespread abuse. It also concluded that the policy was not just wrong but was "genocidal" in that its aim was the disappearance of Aborigines as a distinct group. This conclusion was angrily scorned by some. However, Robert Manne, editor of the journal *Quadrant*, wrote in February 1998: "Even if the charge of genocide remains contentious between people of good will, as I suspect it might, that does nothing to change the fact that the policy of child removal constitutes one of the most shameful, if not the most shameful episode in twentieth-century Australian history."

After some months, the government announced that it would make available $63 million over four years for counseling and family reunion services.

However, it ignored the proposal for a national apology, arguing that it could not be held responsible for the actions of its predecessors. It ignored, too, the concept of a national Sorry Day — a formal and public acknowledgment of past wrong.

On their own initiative, many community groups, Aboriginal and non-Aboriginal, came together and launched a plan to hold a Sorry Day on 26 May 1998, exactly a year after the report had been laid before Parliament. In an article in the Canberra *Times* (April 7, 1998), John Bond, a member of the National Sorry Day Committee, wrote:

> It took us over 20 years to honor our Vietnam veterans because we were ashamed of what we, as a country, had pushed them into. It is taking us longer to honor the stolen generations, because we are even more ashamed. But on Sorry Day we will celebrate them, for there is much to celebrate. Their struggle to overcome their tragic experience has given many of them qualities of resilience, humor, compassion. They are a source of strength for our country.

The idea spread rapidly, with strong backing from churches and from education authorities who produced study material. One community group had already launched "Sorry Books" in which people could express in their own words their sorrow for the forced removal policies. Eventually more than 1,200 such books were distributed, in which some 400,000 people wrote personal messages.

A look through these books conveys a sense of a grieving nation reaching out to its Aboriginal people. Young and old, people of all backgrounds, often taking great effort to write neatly and legibly, express sentiments like "This day means, hopefully, a new start and new hopes for the future." "I don't feel guilt but I certainly feel some shame and sorrow for the hurt." "For the terrible grief of a people, and for the cause of that grief, I am sorry." "I offer my deepest apology for all the years of injustice suffered by your people. Sorry is not enough but this day is appropriate."

Occasionally there crept in a message from someone who resented the whole idea of apology. There were also some digs at the prime minister: "I'm not taking responsibility but I'm definitely saying I'm sorry it happened. John Howard and his government should do at least as much."

One message, illustrated with a flower, was simply signed "From a mother in Canberra." It read, "I am sorry for your pain, and hope the messages this book contains help to heal and bring a better understanding to all Australians of the special culture and heritage native Australians can share. May the gesture found in these pages help to overcome despair and restore hope and love."

On National Sorry Day, the books were handed to elders of the "stolen generations" in hundreds of ceremonies in cities, towns and rural centers. Thousands of churches and schools observed the day. In Perth, West Australia, in the Anglican cathedral, leaders of all the churches read out their denominations' apologies for the "removals." Patrick Dodson, former chairperson of the Council for Aboriginal Reconciliation, told the crowded congregation, "Take confidence, because in the hearts of many young Australians there is a desire to go into the next century with the banner of reconciliation fully unfurled. I can survive without your apology but the integrity of the nation cannot survive without it."

In Adelaide, South Australia, a national monument to the stolen generations was unveiled. The granite carving portrays an empty coolamon, or cradle, with water, representing tears, washing down over the faces of Aborigines who had been taken away from their parents. It is inscribed with words from Fiona's testimony: "And every morning as the sun came up the whole family would wail. They did that for 32 years until they saw me again. Who can imagine what a mother went through? But you have to learn to forgive."

In Melbourne, Victoria, the lord mayor handed the keys of the city to representatives of the stolen generations, and the city churches rang their bells.Two thousand people attended an ecumenical service in St. Paul's Cathedral. A meeting in the Town Hall was chaired by Dimity Fifer, a member of the Council for Aboriginal Reconciliation. She said, "Reconciliation is at times a difficult process, much like the building of any relationship. It is built on listening and it is about hanging in there when we hear things we may find difficult. Listening takes courage and energy and we are rewarded as a nation and as individuals when we make this commitment."

In Sydney, New South Wales, thousands rallied at the Opera House. On a national radio program marking the event, one of the speakers was Avis Gale, who had been taken away from her mother when she was one week old. She accepted the apologies but said that she in turn had some apologizing to do. She was learning to love her enemies. Avis explained that when she and others were invited to receive the apology of the Synod of the Uniting Church in South Australia, "it freaked me out." At the age of eight, in rebellion against the institution in which she had been placed, she threw every Bible she could find onto a bonfire. For this she was told she would go to Hell and, to make the point, the letter H was branded on her leg. The church's apology for its part in the removal policies moved her deeply. She realized that she also had apologies to make. In fact, she agonized over a list of twenty people or so whom she hated most, gradually scrubbing each one off her list with a stubby pencil as she "gave them away." She emerged from victimhood when she realized that there might be some she had hurt who would need to forgive her. "One day they will have to meet their Maker," she said, "but so will I."

State legislatures passed resolutions. The Australian Senate marked the day with a minute's silence, as did every prison in Queensland. Newspapers made it the main subject of their opinion columns and it dominated the radio waves. Special music was composed. Around the country could be heard the haunting refrain of Aborigine singer Archie Roach's song "Took the Children Away."

Lois "Lowitja" O'Donoghue, the first and only Aboriginal to address the United Nations General Assembly, said the day was "a milestone on the road to reconciliation." She is a descendant of the original keepers of Uluru (known in English as Ayers Rock), whose ancestry goes back more than 60,000 years, but she spent the first half of her life as a non-citizen. At the age of two she was taken from her family and, like Avis, did not meet her mother for thirty years. In response to one apology, she said, "We forgive you for the part you played in the removal of children from our mothers, families, culture, our land and our language. But never ask us to forget the pain and anguish we have endured over years."

Four months after the National Sorry Day, the largest dinner party ever to be held in the Great Hall of Parliament House drew 700 public servants, dignitaries, diplomats, politicians, business people, family and friends to "express togetherness." Along with the Aboriginal people, there were representatives of many of the ethnic immigrant peoples of Australia. Australian Immigration and Multi-cultural Affairs Minister Phillip Ruddock called the evening "a turning point in our commitment to cultural diversity."

The chairperson of the Council for Aboriginal Reconciliation, Evelyn Scott, said, "Many Australians, in particular indigenous and Asian Australians, feel the core values of our society are being threatened by ignorance and bigotry, and by people who use us as scapegoats for their own failings. I am so heartened by your attendance here tonight. I am an absolute believer that reconciliation must be a people's movement — and you are living proof of my belief."

On the first anniversary of the Sorry Day, the National Sorry Day Committee invited the whole Australian community to participate in a "Journey of Healing," under the patronage of former Prime Minister Malcolm Fraser and Carol Kendall, chairperson of the Stolen Generations Working Group. It was launched at Uluru, the monolithic rock at the heart of the Australian continent. Reporting on the event, the *Sydney Morning Herald* headlined its story, "Radiating from the Rock, new ritual of hope."

Fraser, who was prime minister from 1975 to 1983, wrote in an article in *The Age* (April 7, 1999), headlined "Why we must say sorry":

Facing the truth about our own past, when it is contrary to that which we have been taught for generations, is difficult. Unless non-Aboriginal Australians are prepared to look at the past honestly there will be no real reconciliation with Aborigines. True reconciliation does not only involve material things — it also involves matters of the spirit. This is where the question of an apology for past wrongs is relevant. An apology does not say "I am guilty." It is a recognition that our society perpetuated a wrong and that we are sorry it happened. It is perhaps the most important thing we can do which is within our power, to address matters of the spirit. An apology is not even a commentary on the morality or ethics of the people involved in policies at the same time. An apology is a criticism of the act much more than a criticism of the people who lived in a different time with different ideas. An apology says that, by today's standards, these things should never have happened.

Gatjil Djerrkura, who heads one of Australia's main Aboriginal organisations, says of the Journey of Healing, "It could inspire a rolling action of initiatives all over the country bringing communities together and encouraging a societal transformation at grassroots level." The Journey emphasizes three aspects: recognition of the injustices of the past, not as a matter of personal guilt, but as a matter of healing wounds by embracing, rather than shunning, Australian history; commitment to deal with the consequences of forced removals — broken families, lost identity, shattered physical and mental health, loss of language, culture and connection to traditional land, and loss of parenting skills; and unity, through listening to each other, both to see the racism, prejudice and hurts which keep us apart and to benefit from everyone's wisdom on how to meet the needs of the whole community.

"Last year the Australian community took the first step by saying 'Sorry'. The next step is to overcome the continuing consequences of the wrong," wrote Bond in *Australian Medicine,* urging doctors to bring their skills to the healing process and encourage community initiatives which can help restore health.

The Journey of Healing is being led by members of the stolen generations who have themselves suffered and are taking the initiative to heal the wounds remaining among people of all races. One of these is Fiona, whose story began this chapter. She says, "The suffering we have endured has made us a strong people, a courageous people, a people of compassion who understand the suffering of others. Don't let bitterness, hate or anger take root in our hearts. Only as we choose to forgive can we be truly healed."

Another woman giving leadership is Audrey Kinnear, a policy advisor on indigenous health to the Aboriginal and Torres Straits Islander Commission in Canberra. In 1998, presenting a copy of the report *Bringing Them Home* to the Caux conference center in Switzerland, she said, "The report is about pain, people, cultural survival, the capacity to say sorry and the capacity to forgive." She had been separated from her family at the age of four and raised in a mission. She was twenty-eight when she met her mother again. For years she didn't know where she belonged, sometimes wishing she were a full-blood Aboriginal, sometimes wishing she were white, because these two were accepted:

But we were half-caste — outcaste in white Australia — we didn't belong anywhere. I know some people have a problem with the words "stolen generation" but it is very appropriate because of what has been stolen from us — our families, our language, our community, our culture, our identity and our sense of belonging. These things can never be made up. But my Aboriginal family helped me to heal. They accepted and understood. National Sorry Day was the final thing in my healing, because it gave recognition to pain. It had other Australians saying "I'm sorry" and it gave us permission to cry and grieve together. Since then I've suddenly become aware that our people aren't victims any more.

On May 26, 1999, the Journey was launched all over the country. In Canberra, a thousand people crowded the Great Hall of

Parliament and finished the meeting by singing together the theme song of the Journey, written by two Aboriginal people:

> Come join the journey, Journey of Healing
> Let the spirit guide us, hand in hand
> Let's walk together into the future
> The time has come to make a stand.
> Let's heal our hearts, let's heal our pain,
> And bring the stolen children home again
> For our native children to trust again
> We must take this journey together as friends.

Australia faces difficult issues, as it grapples with a fair distribution of land between its Aboriginal and non-Aboriginal inhabitants. In many countries, these issues have provoked bitter conflict. The Journey of Healing gives hope that Australians will move beyond the conflict and develop creative solutions that might be of use elsewhere.

On August 27, 1999, two years after he refused to apologize to Aborigines taken from their families, Prime Minister John Howard presented a motion in Parliament that he called an attempt to reconcile black and white Australians. Parliament expressed "its deep and sincere regret that indigenous Australians suffered injustices under the practices of past generations, and for the hurt and trauma that many indigenous people continue to feel." Howard said that Australians should not "embroil themselves in an exercise of shame and guilt" but changed his position on regret. "Without any doubt," he said, "the greatest blemish and stain on the Australian national story is our treatment of the indigenous people. It is important that we recognize that, we confront that, we acknowledge it."

For Yarmuk, Elder of the Ulupna Tribe
buried at Cummeragunja on the Murray, 14th August, 1959

A worn-out body laid in quiet earth,
Attendant trees, a wattle's throb of gold,
The unhurried river hollowing its path,
Wind in the grass — what more is to be told?

You, last of all that knew your tribal tongue,
Rest now with them in this ancestral ground.
Above your grave the towering ancient wrong
Speaks in a silence pregnant and profound.

For named and nameless ills your people bore
From us, who killed by bullet, axe, and pride,
For our stone blindness; for the day we tore
In kindness' name your children from your side,

What could we answer if your ghost should rise
To curse our children's children from the grave?
You rise, but with compassion in your eyes.
Before we knew to ask it, you forgave.

A fire of truth and love was lit in you
Who unembittered fought with bitter fate.
We took the land and life your fathers knew,
You never claimed your heritage of hate,

But poured your life unstinted for the sake
Of those you loved, caught in the world's dark mesh.
Sleep well: but let your burning spirit wake
Till hearts of stone are melted into flesh.

— Michael Thwaites
The Honey Man

4

Beyond the rainbow: Glimpses from the Cape of Good Hope

"I always knew that deep down in every human heart there is mercy and generosity. No one is born hating another person because of the color of his skin, or his background or his religion. People must learn to hate, and if they can learn to hate, they can be taught to love, for love comes more naturally to the human heart than its opposite. Even in the grimmest times in prison, when my comrades and I were pushed to our limits, I would see a glimmer of humanity in one of the guards, perhaps just for a second, but it was enough to reassure me and keep me going."
— Nelson Mandela, South African president, 1994-1999

"South Africa is full of Nelson Mandelas."
— Fazel Randera, Member, Truth and Reconciliation Commission

In the 1980s, few if any people who were knowledgeable about South Africa would have given odds in favor of the country getting as far as it has peacefully as the new century dawns. In fact, there was almost unanimous expectation of a bloodbath. As late as October 1985, the bishop (later archbishop) of Cape Town, Desmond Tutu, who as much as anyone in the public arena had been working for a peaceful solution, warned the UN General Assembly that bloodshed was almost inevitable: "Our country is on the verge of a catastrophe. Only a miracle or the intervention of the West will avert Armageddon."

The word "miracle" has been used freely to describe South Africa's transition from white rule to a multiracial government. "By the standards of today's world, the election in South Africa is a political miracle," wrote Anthony Lewis in the *New York Times*. A year later Queen Elizabeth II, visiting South Africa for the first time in forty-eight years, said, "I have come back to see for myself what is little short of a miracle."

Certainly the carefully crafted political compromises and the imaginative leadership shown by people of all races were contributing factors to a transfer of power in which violence was remarkably absent. Another factor was the establishment of the Truth and Reconciliation Commission, which revealed to the country in almost daily reports the reality that had been long denied.

But another word should be brought to the fore in the story of the new South Africa. It is the word "forgiveness." This is manifest in the capacity of the long-suffering black people in particular to look to the future — a capacity personified for the world in Nelson Mandela. Tutu says, "Had Nelson Mandela and all these others not been willing to forgive, we would not have even reached first base." David Aikman, in his book *Great Souls,* credits Mandela with "the reintroduction of the virtue of forgiveness into the ravaged countryside of twentieth century politics."

After twenty-seven years in prison, eighteen of them on Robben Island, Nelson Mandela took the next step on what he calls in his autobiography his "long walk to freedom":

When I walked out of prison, that was my mission, to liberate the oppressed and the oppressor both. Some say that has now been achieved. But I know that is not the case. The truth is that we are not yet free; we have merely achieved the freedom to be free, the right not to be oppressed. We have not taken the final step of our journey, but the first step on a longer and even more difficult road. For to be free is not merely to cast off one's chains, but to live in a way that respects and enhances the freedom of others. The true test of our devotion to freedom is just beginning.

As Mandela emphasizes, the road ahead is challenging. Forgiveness does not in itself provide jobs or education or answer criminal violence. A Truth and Reconciliation Commission cannot answer corruption or prejudice. But without truth and reconciliation, without forgiveness, the likelihood of the nation having come together to tackle its present problems would be slight.

Another important concept must accompany forgiveness, and this is certainly necessary, many South Africans say, if ongoing reconciliation is to be expected. This is repentance. It is not a fashionable idea in the life of communities; as Brian Frost points out in *Struggling To Forgive,* they prefer to strive for justice or espouse the power of love: "Nevertheless, the practise of repentance, although tough, can provide openings when other avenues are blocked. For genuine repentance clearly implies that a change has already occurred and a new way is desired, different from the old and sweetened maybe by the humility which genuine repentance can bring."

On March 18, 1990, Wilhelm Verwoerd, a grandson of H. F. Verwoerd, the architect of apartheid, wrote a letter to Nelson Mandela:

Dear Mr. Mandela,
This is a personal letter that I have not only wanted to write for a long time, but feel compelled to write. For ages I have wanted to express my thankfulness to you for your inspiring example as a true statesman, and I want to underline my support for your dearly bought ideal of a non-racial democracy in South Africa. In a sense, that is the easy part of this letter.

Since your release the difficult part has become even more difficult. The more I see and read of you, the more I study our country's tragic history, the deeper my realisation of how different everything could have been, of my own people's guilt. And the more painfully I feel the responsibility and guilt of "the one man who would be remembered as the author of our calamity" (Chief Luthuli), namely Dr. H. F. Verwoerd.

Naturally history — a long unjust 27-year-long incarceration and the part my grandfather played in that — can't be changed with a few words. But as an Afrikaner who benefited from apartheid at the expense of other South Africans, as the grandson of the architect of "separate development" — the man who above all others was responsible for your suffering and the suffering of so many other people — I want to say to you: I am very sorry about what happened.

I can't ask for forgiveness on his behalf. In any case, such a request would easily sound meaningless because I understand so little of what you endured during the past few decades. What I can do is to assure you that my wife and I want to spend our lives trying to convert words of apology into deeds. To make South Africa a country of shared, humane freedoms, in place of Verwoerdian "separate freedoms" (for some). I sincerely hope that I will have the opportunity to talk to you personally about this. In the meantime I pray for God's blessings on you, your family and Africa.

The letter published in his autobiography, *My Winds of Change,* was part of Verwoerd's "commitment to reconciliation." As a "white beneficiary of the apartheid system" he was acting "out of a spirit of repentance and restitution."

For some reason the letter never reached Mandela, but later the young Verwoerd had the chance to repeat its contents to him personally. Mandela's first words on meeting Wilhelm were: "How is your grandmother? When you see her again, if she won't mind, would you please convey my best wishes to her. Don't worry about the past. Let us work together for a better future. As a Verwoerd you have a great advantage, when you speak, the people will listen."

To reach this openness to new ideas has been and continues to be for Wilhelm Verwoerd a long walk, too — a "little trek" he calls it, a journey of learning for one brought up in the aura of Afrikanerdom. It has meant a willingness to risk relationships. Various events helped broaden his horizons and depart from "familiar certainties."

In 1988 Verwoerd went with a group of ten other Stellenbosch University students and lecturers to Malawi, Zambia, and Zimbabwe. He had gone regarding himself as an African, with his roots and mother tongue firmly embedded in the continent, and this conviction was strengthened by the moving way they had been welcomed by fellow Africans in all three countries. He learned on this trip, he wrote later, that human dignity was not necessarily destroyed by simplicity, and that he had been influenced by disinformation and negative propaganda about these countries. He was also made aware of the arrogance of his judgments, of his biased and limited understanding of the situation. "Mental capacity, statesmanship, economic initiative," he wrote in *Freeway* in 1989, "are not directly related to race and ethnicity."

Verwoerd returned from the visit concerned that the lack of outward-looking statesmanship and a preoccupation with political and cultural differences on the part of white South Africans were threatening to pull the continent apart: "In the fishbowl of white politics and in the oases of wealth created by apartheid and ethnic socialism, we white South Africans are oblivious to the harm this is causing to fellow-Africans, and are unaware that we are impoverishing ourselves." He recognized that the struggle was fundamentally a conflict of values, "directed not against all white South Africans but against policies and a state perceived as dehumanizing and illegitimate." To break the current dilemmas, idealistic, imaginative, bold statesmanship was needed, and "informed, unselfish, personal commitment to non-racial, 'inclusive' democracy."

While studying in the Netherlands and as a Rhodes Scholar at Oxford in 1986, Verwoerd had already been exposed to ideas and indeed books that were hard to find at home. It took him time, for instance, to be willing to read Donald Woods's book about Steve Biko, the leader of the Black Consciousness Movement, who died in South African police detention in 1977. At Oxford, Verwoerd was ostracized because of his name. Back at home, he read all he could about his grandfather and noted that in 120 books and theses about him, there was no criticism, and no blacks were quoted. On the twenty-fifth anniversary of his grandfather's death in 1991, he put down some notes for an interview, as recorded in *My Winds of Change:*

> Basically the policy of separate development boils down to the fact that good intentions and high-sounding goals were used to justify immoral means. The injustices that sprang from this unholy alliance also desecrated the goals and intentions ...
>
> This warning is terribly relevant for today, but the moral heritage of Dr. Verwoerd to me also signifies that we Afrikaners in particular must admit that his policy was not purely a tactical practical mistake but a moral transgression, that we also have dirt on our hands. This is why we have a responsibility, a moral obligation not to trek away to deserted wastelands, but to stay here and get our hands clean, in a shattered community.

In 1992, Wilhelm Verwoerd joined the African National Congress (ANC), the party of Nelson Mandela; his wife, Melanie, is an ANC member of Parliament. This was too much for his father, who branded his son "a traitor." In 1994 when his grandfather's statue was removed in Bloemfontein, Wilhelm could understand why Afrikaners like his father were upset, but he held firm. He ends his autobiography:

> Even though "white" stands, rightly, for many wrongs, even though many white males are responsible for great injustices, even though white male Afrikaners and racism, sexism and tribalism are often closely linked, even though

white, male Afrikaner Christians have justified these evils, even though a white, male Afrikaner with the initials HF and the surname Verwoerd has become, for most people, the personification of Grand Apartheid, it is not wrong for me to be, amongst other things, a white, male, Afrikaner Christian; I need not even be ashamed to carry the surname Verwoerd. For the question is: What am I doing with these sources of myself? How do I transform being a Christian, white, male, Afrikaner Verwoerd from seductive reasons for destructive self-rejection to creative resources for reconstruction and true reconciliation?

Wilhelm Verwoerd, who is a lecturer in political philosophy and applied ethics at Stellenbosch University and was for a time a researcher with the Truth and Reconciliation Commission, believes that the forgiveness shown by Mandela to whites has a downside in that it "prevents our having to face up to what we have done." He says, "People need to have the pain acknowledged by those perceived to have inflicted the pain." He feels that further repentance is called for, with the emphasis shifting to "concrete acts of restitution."

In November 1990 an event took place that may have contributed significantly to the white population's acceptance of a new political system in South Africa — particularly in regard to the vital role of the churches and faith communities in the reconciliation process. A hotel outside Rustenburg, northwest of Johannesburg, was the site of the first conference in thirty years to bring together the leadership of the white Dutch Reformed Church and all the other South African churches. At the meeting were 230 church leaders from 80 denominations; it was probably the most widely representative gathering of church leaders in South Africa's history. Archbishop Tutu said, "If anyone had predicted in September 1989 that in November 1990 virtually all the churches in South Africa would be gathered together in a national conference, most of us would have been looking for a good psychiatrist for that madman."

Tutu, who in 1984 was awarded the Nobel Peace Prize, told the gathering that those who had wronged others must be ready to make what amends they can: "If I have stolen your pen, I can't really be contrite when I say, 'Please forgive me,' if at the same time I still keep your pen. If I am truly repentant, then I will demonstrate this genuine repentance by returning your pen. Then reconciliation, which is always costly, will happen."

Responding, Willie Jonker, a respected professor of theology at Stellenbosch University, departed from his text to "confess before you and before the Lord, not only my own sin and guilt, and my personal responsibility for the political, social, economic and structural wrongs that have been done to many of you and the results [from] which you and our whole country are still suffering, but vicariously I dare also to do that in the name of the NGK [the Dutch Reformed Church] of which I am a member, and for the Afrikaans people as a whole."

Archbishop Tutu responded spontaneously:

> Professor Jonker made a statement that certainly touched me and I think touched others of us when in public he made a confession and asked to be forgiven. God has brought us to this moment, and I just want to say to you, I am deeply humbled, and I speak only for myself. I cannot, when someone says, "Forgive me," say "I do not." For then I cannot pray the prayer that we prayed: "Forgive us, as we forgive"... but my church has to confess, too. My church has to confess its racism. I have to confess as a black person. How many times have I treated others in my own community as if they were less than the children of God? What is my share in our common sin?

Later in the week the meeting adopted a document called the Rustenburg Declaration. It states: "With a broken and contrite spirit, we ask the forgiveness of God and of our fellow South Africans. We call upon the members of our churches to make this confession their own. We call upon the Government of South Africa to join us in a public confession of guilt and a statement of repentance of wrongs perpetrated over the years."

Methodist Bishop Stanley Mogoba, who conducted the final worship service at Rustenburg, had come to the Christian faith while a prisoner on Robben Island. At Rustenburg he described his ordeal and urged that the forces of hatred and racism in the country be removed by God as they had been in him. In a later television interview on the occasion of his receiving the World Methodist Peace Prize, Mogoba said, "On Robben Island it was difficult to forgive the people who were doing so much to you. However, feelings of anger eat you up more than the other person."

Between 1974 and 1994 there were about fifteen truth commissions in the world — for example, in Bolivia, Chile, Argentina, El Salvador, Uganda, Chad, Ethiopia, Rwanda, and Germany. Some were sponsored by the UN, and some by nongovernmental organisations. Immediately after the inauguration of Nelson Mandela in 1994, the Government of National Unity announced its intention to set up the South African Truth and Reconciliation Commission as a necessary way to help reconcile the nation to its violent past. A year later it came into being through an act of Parliament, with a fourfold agenda: the establishment of as complete a picture of the past as possible; the possible granting of amnesty for crimes committed during the anti-apartheid struggle; the restoration of the human and civil dignity of victims; and the compilation of a report of what went on as well as recommending reparations. Seventeen commissioners were appointed. The act and its preamble recognized the need for reconciliation and reconstruction; for understanding, not vengeance; and for reparation, not retaliation. Archbishop Tutu, who headed the Commission, called it a compromise "between those who want amnesia and those who want retribution." Opening the first session, he said, "One lesson we should be able to teach the world, and that we should be able to teach the people of Bosnia, Rwanda, and Burundi, is that we are ready to forgive."

After two years of hearings, costing some $30 million, the Commission issued a 3,500-page report, recording nearly 20,000 statements about human rights violations. Not everyone who gave evidence experienced healing and reconciliation. Yet, the report concluded, there were cases "where an astonishing willingness to forgive was displayed, where those responsible for violations apologised and committed themselves to a process of restitution, and where the building or rebuilding of relationships was initiated."

The report is a wonderful document, wrote Andreas Whittam Smith in the London *Independent*, using a favorite adjective of Archbishop Tutu: "Wonderful? Yes, because of the grace and wisdom with which Tutu conducted the controversial hearings; yes, because of the nobility displayed in some of the evidence; yes, even though the report relentlessly documents harrassment, torture and killing, often depicting, in Hannah Arendt's chilling phrase, the 'banality of evil.'" He says that where the Commission's work is "truly ground-breaking" is in facilitating reconciliation.

Daily, the hearings had been broadcast to the nation, transmitting into people's homes gruesome stories of torture, but also amazing stories of forgiveness. Archbishop Tutu was often in tears. He said, "It never ceases to astonish me the magnanimity of many victims who suffered the most heinous of violations, who reach out to embrace their tormentors with joy, willing to forgive and wanting to reconcile."

There were some who would not own up to their misdeeds under questioning; there were others who would not forgive. A small percentage of those who applied for amnesty were granted it. Steve Biko's mother had said before she died, "Yes, I would forgive my son's killers. I am a Christian, and we Christians do forgive. But first I must know who to forgive and what to forgive, which means I must be told fully what happened and why." The prison officers who were questioned about Biko's death were felt by the Commission to have lied and were not given amnesty.

Perhaps the most gruesome evidence was given by a security policeman, Jeffrey Benzien, when he demonstrated his "wet-bag torture" to Commission members. Ashley Forbes, who was tortured by him, was in tears at the sight. But soon afterward, there was a *Sunday Times* headline "I forgive torture cop, says Forbes." The former political prisoner is quoted: "That picture of Benzien showed me what the Truth and Reconciliation Commission can achieve. It brought to light in a vivid manner what both Benzien and I went through and helped heal us both. I forgive him and I feel sorry for him. Now I can get on with the rest of my life." Forbes qualified his forgiveness, though, by stating that it would be stretching things too far to say that he had been "reconciled" with his former torturer. At Benzien's amnesty hearing, they shook hands.

In an article assessing this event, headlined "Forgive the torturer, not the torture," Wilhelm Verwoerd pointed out that the main beneficiary of forgiveness is not Benzien, but Forbes:

> He is forgiving his torturer. This is possible because he has been able to look beyond the torture and see Benzien the human being and "feel sorry for him." In the words of another survivor, Tony Yengeni, he is able to see "the man behind the wet bag." That is central to Archbishop Tutu's call for people to forgive. It is a call to recognize the humanity of "perpetrators" even if their humanity is hidden behind a wet bag.

The report stated that "the evidence of those who have given witness (is) that, by telling their story, they have shared a burden and found a new sense of peace. This is very obvious from the sheer look of some of them as they walk out of the meetings of the Commission."

Lucas Sikwepere, who had been blinded by a bullet and tortured, said after speaking, "I feel that what has been making me sick all the time is the fact that I couldn't tell my story. But now it feels like I got my sight back by coming here and telling you the story." A conscript who was tortured said, " It is almost as if the silence is ending, as if we are waking up from a long bad nightmare." An Indian who had once dreamed of going into Parliament and shooting every white cabinet minister told the Commission, "I grew to realize that hate is a boomerang that circles back and hurts you."

There were some memorable encounters.

Beth Savage, badly injured by a bomb, expressed a wish to meet the man that threw the grenade "in an attitude of forgiveness and hope that he could forgive me too for whatever reason." She had the chance to do so later. After meeting with the man, an Azanian People's Liberation Army commander, she said she no longer had nightmares about the attack. A former South African Air Force captain, Neville Clarence, also blinded in an attack, shook hands before the hearing with Aboobaker Ismail, the ANC man who had planned it. "I don't hold any grudges," said Clarence. An editorial in the *Sowetan* said, "Clarence's magnanimous gesture will no doubt stand out as a symbol of hope for a society that remains deeply divided."

Evaluating the significance of the Commission, Judge Richard A. Goldstone, who was chief prosecutor at the UN International Criminal Tribunal, said, "One only has to imagine where South Africa would be today but for the Truth and Reconciliation Commission in order to appreciate what it has achieved." He described its work as "an essential resource for anyone interested in finding a means of curbing war crimes and human rights abuses in the next millennium." (Another story from the Commission appears in chapter 11 of this book.)

Just as Wilhelm Verwoerd has been for the moment disowned by some of his family and people, so some blacks had to persist despite criticism from their peers, criticism directed particularly at those who were dedicated to nonviolence before the white government had been dislodged. They had the faith before it seemed possible that one day blacks would run South Africa. Two early men of courage were William Nkomo and Philip Vundla, and both were helped to move beyond a racist approach by the actions and words of Afrikaners who had recognized that they and their people needed to change.

William Nkomo was a medical doctor in Atteridgeville and the first black president of the South African Race Relations Institute. At Fort Hare he gained the first of his three university degrees and became politically conscious. In 1938 he was chosen to represent South Africa at the first World Youth Peace Congress in the United States, but his passport application was turned down.

At Witwatersrand University, he was the first African member of the Student Representative Council. He joined the African National Congress and then, along with others like Nelson Mandela who felt that the organization was not militant enough, founded the African National Congress Youth League. "We felt that older people were going too hat in hand to the authorities and wanted a more dynamic and militant organisation to fight for the freedom and independence of black people." He was dedicated to bloodshed, to revolution, and to driving the white man into the sea.

Then Nkomo met a group of Afrikaner theological students from Pretoria University who told him they had been wrong to adopt an attitude of racial superiority and described their commitment to a different South Africa — their desire to find a basis of unity through listening to the voice of conscience on the principle not of who is right, but of what is right. "They seemed so sincere. It seemed senseless to liquidate such people and reactionary for me to maintain the old stand," said Nkomo. "What shook me most was to meet rabid Afrikaner nationalists who had found something bigger to live for and were prepared to apologize to me and other African nationalists for their former attitude of hatred and arrogance. I began to realise that instead of planning the liquidation of people, I could sit with them, and listen to God's guidance, to plan for a new South Africa together with them."

In 1954 Nkomo spoke at a public meeting in Cape Town City Hall. He said, "I swore to drive the white man to the sea. Then I saw white men change and I saw black men change. And I myself decided to change. I'm now fighting with thousands of Africans for a hate-free, fear-free, greed-free continent peopled by free men and women."

One of the Afrikaner nationalists, George Daneel, a Dutch Reformed Church minister and former Springbok rugby player, spoke along with him.

Over the next years Nkomo and Daneel worked together. Blacks sometimes accused Nkomo of being a sell-out, while whites accused Daneel of softening up the Afrikaners so that the blacks could take over. Some of Nkomo's opponents even tried to set his house on fire. Daneel was attacked by H. F. Verwoerd in the

Cabinet and by the Afrikaner secret society, the Broederbond. But many also followed them in their broader nonracial approach. The town of Atteridge organized a day to honor Nkomo as he continued to speak out on issues affecting his people.

A Pretoria policeman stopped Nkomo for a traffic offense and hit him in the face, seriously injuring his eye. The traffic officer was brought to court, where the magistrate found him guilty but discharged the case. Bitterness again welled up in Nkomo, and some urged him to seek revenge. "I remember saying we had taken too many things to God and perhaps this we should take to blood. When I went home God spoke to me clearly that this was the action of an individual and I shouldn't blame it on a people."

Nkomo died in 1972 at age fifty-seven. Ten thousand people came to his funeral. Alex Boraine, president of the Methodist Conference and later to be vice chairman of the Truth and Reconciliation Commission, said of him, "Every experience of suffering which his people bore, he felt in his own body and spirit. He knew no hatred for any man, yet his indictment of injustice was a hurricane of fire."

His Afrikaner friend, George Daneel, spoke at his funeral:

> When I heard him say that he had shed his hatred and bitterness towards the white man, I realized that it was the attitude of superiority and the arrogance of white men like myself which had caused the bitterness and hatred in the hearts of black men. I asked God to forgive me and I apologized publicly. It may be that every white man in this country, maybe every white man in the world, needs to face up to this. Since then I've committed myself, with many others of all races, to put right what is wrong in this country.

Philip (P. Q.) Vundla, who all his life was at the heart of the struggles of the African people on the gold-mining reef of Transvaal, was a close friend of William Nkomo, and like him was deeply influenced by the change he perceived in Afrikaners.

As a young man working in the mines outside Johannesburg, Vundla watched the funeral of a child and thought,

"Terrible if I died before I have done in enough whites." He became a full-time organizer for the African Mineworkers Union and in 1952 was elected to the national executive council of the African National Congress. He wrote for the *Bantu World*. He used to say to his people, "The only good white man is a dead white man."

One day Vundla was visited by a young nationalist Afrikaner, Nico Ferreira, who worked for the Native Affairs Department. He had been secretary of the students at a leading Afrikaans university. When Vundla heard that Ferreira was waiting to see him, his reaction was, "I wonder what he wants. No good news ever came from a white man." The only reason he expected a visit from whites was to be arrested. But Ferreira told him that he had been sent to work in his area and wanted to pay his respects. He said, "I have decided to give up my old ways of thinking and start living differently so that a man like you can begin to trust me."

Vundla was struck by his sincerity and humility. Ferreira's life had been deeply affected by meeting Nkomo and by his view that any idea that excludes anyone else is too small for the age in which we live. After a long talk with Nkomo, he had realized that he had to be different.

Vundla, like Nkomo, now began to take a more independent line. An issue arose over a strike of schoolteachers called by African nationalist leaders. He thought it was wrong because the children would suffer, and he spoke against it. As a result, he was stabbed by members of an African National Congress Youth League branch he himself had founded. Vundla was able to joke, "Even the people who assaulted me were my trainees." From his hospital bed, he said, "They may kill me, but they will never kill the idea for which I stand." His supporters wanted to hit back, but he called a meeting after leaving hospital to say, "Revenge is not the way." Several years later, one of the men who stabbed him came to him and they were reconciled.

Vundla continued to serve on the ANC executive and was later elected chairman of the advisory board, representing 600,000 Africans in the townships of Johannesburg. When he died, a cortège of 250 cars and ten buses followed his coffin. "I learnt that what you achieve by violence you will need greater violence to maintain," he liked to say. "Those who say that bloodshed is the answer have other people's blood in mind, not their own." And on another occasion: "The laws are unbearable and must be changed. But it is important to change people as well as laws."

Two days before his death, Vundla was still wrestling with officialdom, fighting for the cause of African widows threatened with dispossession of their houses. He had the courage to pursue a hate-free policy before his people were free. South African journalist Anthony Duigan says that the pioneering work of Vundla and Nkomo "established a platform for the modern proponents of forgiveness as the basis of reconciliation."

A friend of Nkomo and Vundla, Motlalepula Chabaku, carried on their legacy in the new South Africa as speaker of the legislative assembly of the Free State and later a member of Parliament. She says of Vundla, "We thought at first that he would become soft. But no! He became stronger because he was clear in himself, and wanted nothing for himself." She adds, "South Africa needs leaders like Nkomo and Vundla who will not be bought by selfish, personal ambition. Hate is not the most effective way. So many of us hate each other because of our positions, because you oppose me. This makes us slaves of those we hate. No, the very person you hate is the person you have got to win."

Nico Ferreira, the young nationalist who had such an effect on Vundla's life, has stayed true to his conviction. In his work the process of repentance and forgiveness has meant a totally new approach to development. Ferreira and his wife, Loel, who comes from the English-speaking community, realized that if reconciliation was to become a reality, the basic problems of poverty, unemployment, and education had to be addressed. Since 1973 they have been helping Africans create and run their own businesses. In 1990, following a period of conflict, unrest, and boycotts, they encouraged their community of Stutterheim to come together to initiate a process of reconciliation tied in with rural enterprise development and self-employment and to set up the Stutterheim Business Advice Center. Money was raised to provide business advice, loans, and encouragement for black Africans to become rural entrepreneurs in small shops, construction work, and other enterprises, and to get the needed training. When apartheid ended and the new government came in, this work was in place and is strongly encouraged by it.

When the Stutterheim Center was first set up, the economy of this area of about 50,000 people was dying. A consumer boycott had closed fourteen businesses; living conditions for the black majority were poor; and relations between the races were characterized by suspicion and distrust. Under apartheid education of blacks had been limited to the lower grades. Moreover, a legacy of the boycotts in the 1980s was a rejection of education, with youths refusing to attend school and parents dubious of the need for it.

A process of discussion, the Stutterheim Forum, led to the realization that if the reconciliation process was to be hastened, these basic problems of poverty, unemployment, and education had to be addressed. This led to the establishment of a nonprofit development foundation, which in a short time initiated thirty-five projects covering a wide range of needs. Schools are now being built with government help. One Stutterheim project is preschool creches where mothers in the townships work with the teachers to prepare young children for school and help with day care.

Reviewing the Stutterheim experience, David Dewar, professor of architecture and planning at the University of Cape Town, says that the most important achievements are not reflected in the projects undertaken but in the tangible growth in trust, confidence, and management capacity of the people who have been involved in the process: "Strong friendships have been forged in a previously deeply divided and distrustful community."

The Stutterheim Forum is regarded as a model by many similar rural communities in South Africa. The development process there has gone from conflict resolution to dialogue, and then to the implementation of development initiatives. Inquiries from other communities indicate the interest in learning from the Stutterheim strategy. The Forum has developed a manual to provide guidelines for rural communities to initiate and manage a development program. It is a guide, not a blueprint, they say — "a shared vision supported by imagination and innovation" — and a response to people's needs.

An article in the *Los Angeles Times* (May 28, 1999) assessed what had been achieved in Stutterheim:

> In the Border farming and logging town, named after a 19th century German army commander once stationed here, the racial divide is also looking remarkably unlike the colonial past. A rapprochement is underway that has blacks and whites working hand in hand for the first time. All is not well by any measure, but in the vast landscape of racial disharmony that is South Africa, the 30,000 residents here stand out: Blacks and whites acknowledge that they cannot go it alone; their destinies are one and the same.

Barbara Nussbaum, who has described the Stutterheim development in her book *Making a Difference,* believes that political issues are confronted through and moderated by the development process and may result in less polarized positions. She writes, "While it is necessary to confront political and other deep-rooted suspicions resulting from the past, these should not prevent developmental advances which improve the quality of life of the people occurring as rapidly as possible: while confronting the past, it is necessary to move forward."

Assessing South Africa's commitment to reconciliation, Brian Frost writes in *Struggling To Forgive:*

> South Africa has moved into the future with one leap forward, developing a politics of forgiveness in a more sophisticated manner than any other country. It now needs to show how citizens can be empowered to join in that process at the grass-roots and help create a multi-faith and multi-cultural society across all the former divisions. If it begins to do this it may well become one of the key players in the twenty-first century.

5

After Good Friday

"What keeps me going is that more and more of our women, both Roman Catholic and Protestant, are telling the men that it is better to sit around a table and talk than stand around a graveyard and cry. Those tears are not colored in orange and green. They are tears of sorrow. I never believe in judging a man by the church he attends on Sunday or the color of his skin, but by his character. It is not being a Roman Catholic or a Protestant which will create peace. It is being a Christian. Peace is not going to be achieved either by the politicians or the army. It is going to be done by personal contact."

— Saidie Patterson, *All Her Paths Are Peace: Women Pioneers in Peacemaking*

"I not saying 'Forgive and forget,' I'm saying 'Remember and repent.'"

— Canon Nicholas Frayling

On November 11, 1998, a remarkable ceremony took place in Belgium at Messines, scene of a crucial battle in World War I. In 1917 it was a strategic location held by the Germans but attacked and overrun by soldiers of the British Army, who at that point of the front came largely from the 16th Irish and 36th Ulster divisions.

It is one of the ironies of history in Ireland that more Irish died fighting for Britain than in Ireland's own war of independence or the civil war that followed. Nearly 250,000 Irishmen volunteered to fight with Britain in World War I. Fifty thousand of them died. "As the heroes of Ireland's independence were seizing the General Post Office and facing the British Army at Easter 1916," wrote Charles Glass in 1995, "most Irishman of their generation, Catholic and Protestant, were wearing British khaki and marching under the Union flag in France. To accept that fact is to begin to understand the nature of Ireland and its hesitation to embrace the unity and independence of the entire island."

The ceremony at Messines marked the first time the Irish State had honored those quarter million, largely forgotten Irishmen who served in the British forces in the Great War. The monument is a 110-foot Irish round tower made with 400 metric tons of stone taken from the former Mullingar workhouse. The president of Ireland, Mary McAleese, unveiled the monument, watched by Queen Elizabeth and the king and queen of Belgium.

Mayor Jean Liefooghe of Mesen (the Belgian spelling of Messines) expressed the hope that that new monument would make visitors reflect on the stupidity of violence and war. The *Irish Times,* reporting the event under the headline "History made again on Flanders Field," wrote, "As far as conflict between the Irish was concerned, there was already some evidence of that reflection. In the village square the pipers of the band of the Royal Irish Regiment, once the Ulster Defence Regiment so detested by nationalists, swapped tunes with the Army Number One band with which it had merged for the occasion."

The *Irish Times* writer said that the best speech on this day of few speeches came from the former loyalist leader Glenn Barr, who with former Donegal member of Parliament Paddy Harte, founded the Journey of Reconciliation Trust which built the monument. Barr asked people to think of the young work trainees from North and South who had helped to build it as a force for reconciliation, and he expressed the hope that never again would any young person on the island of Ireland have to die for Ireland. "This little poppy, " he said, "offers no offense to anyone, yet we have made it a symbol of division back in Ireland." He asked "Catholic Ireland" to wear it in future "in order that the spirits of these young heroes which have haunted this battlefield for more than eighty years can finally be laid to rest."

Another remarkable event for Ireland was the speech that same year to the Irish Parliament by Tony Blair — the first speech ever by a British prime minister in Dublin. Addressing a joint session of the Irish Senate and House of Representatives which was broadcast live to the country, Blair said that down through the centuries, Ireland and Britain had inflicted too much pain on each other, and now, as two modern countries, they could try to put their histories behind them and "try to forgive and forget those age-old enmities." He spoke of "so much shared history, so much shared pain. And now the shared hope of a new beginning." He was not asking for anyone to surrender, but for everyone to declare the victory of peace: "We need not be prisoners of our history. We can understand the emotions generated by Northern Ireland's troubles, but we cannot really believe, as we approach the twenty-first century, there is not a better way forward to the future than murder, terrorism and sectarian hatred." The speaker of the Irish Parliament, Seamus Pattison, described the speech as a significant step forward in the maturing relationship between Britain and Ireland.

Two other significant steps on the road to this Irish speech were Prime Minister Blair's expression of regret, shortly after his election, for the way Britain failed the Irish people in the famine that claimed more than a million lives 150 years earlier, and his reopening the inquiry into "Bloody Sunday," the tragic event twenty-five years before when fourteen civilians in Derry were killed by British paratroopers.

For many years, the continuing divisions in Northern Ireland between two groups who both claim to be Christians have been a reproach to Christians everywhere, with cruelty on both sides and more than three thousand people killed and thirty thousand injured in a quarter century. But on Good Friday of 1998, an agreement was signed in East Belfast which was overwhelmingly endorsed by referenda on both sides of the border. Enough progress toward a settlement had been made that the Nobel Peace Prize for 1998 was awarded to the Northern Irish political leaders David Trimble and John Hume. The agreement should also be attributed in part to the women of Northern Ireland who have helped keep the peace process alive. A bombing in the village of Omagh shortly afterward served to underline how precarious any agreement must be if one does not deal with the bitterness of the years — as did the failure a year later to implement all its provisions.

In the last quarter century it is the setbacks, like Omagh, that have tended to garner the headlines. But this has been a period of more cross-sectarian initiatives than ever in Irish history, with Protestants praying for Catholics and Catholics praying for Protestants, and more organizations and groups becoming identi-fied with the peace process and engaging in honest dialogue across the historic divide. Well known initiatives include Corrymeela, the Christian Renewal Centre at Rostrevor, and the Columbanus Community of Reconciliation, all in the North, and the Glencree Centre for Reconciliation in the Republic.

Again and again, the setbacks have inspired steps forward. In 1987, for instance, an Irish Republican Army bomb exploded in Enniskillen on Remembrance Day, killing eleven Protestants at their annual war memorial service. In Ireland's bomb-filled history, it was not the worst of outrages, but there was an element to it that reached people in both Protestant and Catholic communities, in both Northern Ireland and the Republic, and in Britain, stirring emotions deeper than hate and revenge. Irish Prime Minister Charles Haughey supported a call by the combined churches for a minute of silence in the Republic in memory of the bomb victims. An AP dispatch reported that the "revulsion felt throughout the island over the slaughter of innocents at prayer has forged a determination that it will never happen again."

The public feeling was profoundly influenced by the televised interview of bombing victim Gordon Wilson, who had lain under the rubble with his twenty-year-old daughter, Marie, and held her hand as she died. "I bear no ill will," he said the next day. He and his wife, Joan, sought not revenge but peace. "She had been screaming at me, then reassuring me," he said of Marie. "'Daddy, I love you very much.' Those were the last words she spoke. Marie's last words were of love. It would be no way for me to remember her by having words of hatred in my mouth."

A *New York Times* correspondent wrote, "In part because of Gordon Wilson's ability to articulate the personal grief so often overlooked in political violence, the bombing is being cited and pondered more than the usual Irish violence." Queen Elizabeth II, in her Christmas message that year, quoted Wilson and said everyone had been moved by his words. BBC viewers voted him Man of the Year.

After his TV appearance the bereaved father received 5,000 letters of support from around the world. From Dublin, the lord mayor brought books of condolence with 45,000 signatures from the Republic. Cardinal Thomas O'Fiaich, Roman Catholic Primate of All Ireland, appeared on television and asked forgiveness of all Protestants. Brian Hannon, the Protestant bishop whose diocese includes Enniskillen, spoke at a memorial service in Dublin: "May God forgive us, individually and as communities, for actions and attitudes of ours that have contributed to the violence or anger which leads to it."

Heartening initiatives followed the tragedy, such as the annual bursaries sponsored by both the British and Canadian governments which allow young Catholics and Protestants together to visit communities in other countries. These visits are known as "the spirit of Enniskillen." They go a long way to demonstrating Gordon Wilson's belief that out of great evil an even greater good can follow.

Sadly, the hope expressed that it would never happen again was not to be. In 1993 the Provisional IRA planted a bomb in

Warrington, England, which killed two children and wounded fifty people (for Warrington's response, see chapter 11). There was again a spontaneous outpouring of sympathy and support, from throughout Britain but also from Ireland. Two hundred thousand people in Ireland signed books of condolence. Gordon Wilson, by then a senator in the Irish Parliament, came to Warrington to share the grief.

The Warrington tragedy was also the catalyst for an initiative from the rector of Liverpool, Nicholas Frayling. It was the third in a series of events that catapulted him into action.

In 1979, when Earl Mountbatten, a respected member of Britain's royal family, was assassinated by Irish terrorists, Canon Frayling had a moment of awareness. He realized that there would be no peace in Ireland until there was an expression of sorrow on the part of Britain for all the hurt and injustice which had been done to the Irish people over hundreds of years. He kept this thought, however, to himself.

In May 1985, twenty-seven people died in Heysel, Belgium, in a riot after a soccer match between Liverpool and the Italian team Juventus. Their deaths were blamed on some of Liverpool's fans at the game. "We have accepted the events in Brussels as a national disgrace of which we all have reason to be ashamed," concluded the *Sunday Telegraph*. "It is well that we have done so." Another London Sunday paper, the *Observer*, commented, "Football hooliganism has finally brought our national game to its knees, and the burden of dealing with the problem now belongs to the entire nation."

Two positive initiatives from Liverpool did much to heal what could have been a lasting and deep bitterness and antagonism between Italy and Britain. These were services in the city's two cathedrals and the visit of a civic delegation to Turin. Frayling, then a canon at Liverpool's Anglican Cathedral, helped to arrange a "Service of Sorrow and Penitence, in Hope of Reconciliation" that drew more than two thousand people on a Saturday morning. While the choir sang "God Be in My Head and in My Understanding," the lord lieutenant of Merseyside presented to the ambassadors of Italy and Belgium silver salvers inscribed "To the people of Italy (Belgium), a token of deep sorrow and sympathy." The Anglican bishop preached; the moderator of the Free Churches and the Catholic archbishop led prayers; children lit candles as a symbol of the hope of reconciliation; and the service ended with the Prayer of St. Francis.

Prayer of St. Francis

Lord, make me an instrument of your peace.
Where there is hatred, let me sow love;
Where there is injury, pardon;
Where there is doubt, faith;
Where there is despair, hope;
Where there is darkness, light;
Where there is sadness, joy.

O Divine Master, grant that I may seek
not so much to be consoled as to console;
To be understood as to understand;
To be loved as to love;
For it is in giving that we receive;
It is in pardoning that we are pardoned,
And it is in dying that we are born to eternal life.
Amen.

Both ambassadors spoke of the powerful effect of the service. The Italian ambassador said afterward in a BBC interview, "You have done more than was needed. The Italian people will forgive." The Belgian ambassador asked, "Why have you done this? This terrible thing was not Liverpool's fault." The Catholic archbishop, who had said a special mass in his cathedral a week before, commented, "The mass was a time for tears. This is a new beginning."

The Liverpool civic delegation that went to Turin included representatives from all political parties and both soccer clubs, the editor of the main paper, the Anglican bishop and the Catholic archbishop. The archbishop said a mass in Italian, though his knowledge of the language is limited. The editor took with him copies of his paper published in Italian, apologizing for what had happened. The day the Liverpool party returned home, the Italian daily, *Tutto Sport,* had the headline, "Liverpool, Turin forgives you." .

As Canon Frayling saw the healing ripples from this humble move by Liverpool, his earlier thought about Ireland came once more to the fore. He later observed, "The Heysel service made a deep impression on me at the time. It was to have a profound effect on my life and ministry for many years to come."

Two years later, Frayling was made rector of Liverpool. The Parish of Liverpool comprises most of the city center and the area of Vauxhall by the docks. The latter neighborhood is where thousands of destitute Irish emigrants came to settle in the years following the great famine of the 1840s. Lacking resources and physical strength, many died where they landed. The population of that part of the parish remains about 95 percent Roman Catholic. "You can't be rector of Liverpool in the Church of England," he says, "without being deeply concerned about Ireland, because, without Ireland and the Irish, Liverpool would just not be Liverpool."

Then, in March 1993, came the bomb in Warrington. The combination of the earlier incident on Merseyside and the reconciling response from thousands in the Republic to this latest bomb attack seemed to provide, the canon says, the moment he had been waiting for since the death of Mountbatten fourteen years before; it was time to express his deepest convictions publicly. He wrote a letter to the London *Independent* in which he praised those demonstrating for peace in Ireland but also called on the people of Britain to recognize the historical background and their responsibilities. He recalled his city's close connections with Ireland, and the fact that in its parochial cemetery 100,000 victims of the famine lay in unmarked graves. He said that it was never too late to say "sorry," even at the risk of inviting accusations of handing victory to terrorists. He asked whether, collectively or individually, his people could find ways of making amends for the past, in order that a political solution might be achieved by consensus.

The response to his words encouraged him. They included a letter, published in the newspaper, by a former chief of staff of the UK Land Forces, Major General Morgan Llewellyn, who wrote, "It is not a weakness but a strength to admit the errors of history and to exorcize the past so as to be able to work for reconciliation in partnership." The canon received more than two hundred letters from around the country.

A few months later, Frayling was invited to speak at a public meeting in Dublin sponsored by the Irish National Congress. He went partly because he felt it was important to hear all sides of the Northern Ireland question. He was encouraged by meeting students who were eager to do just that and whose historical studies had been as one-sided as they claimed his were. "They were willing to face with courage some of the pain, and to welcome into their midst a stranger from a very different tradition. It was a worthwhile expedition, and a very good omen."

Frayling was also invited to speak at a conference in Richmond, Virginia, where Americans were trying to deal with the legacy of slavery. He found the parallels with Britain and Ireland striking. "Unwillingness to face up to our shared history, in all its complexity, means that people and communities are locked into systems of prejudice, mistrust and low or non-existent expectation. It becomes impossible to think or speak well of the other." In Richmond he took part with hundreds of others in a "walk through history," which he describes as "a life-changing experience."

In May 1994 Canon Frayling began four months of study leave, spent largely in Ireland. Out of this came his book, *Pardon and Peace,* which is a carefully reasoned but passionate plea for Britain to approach Ireland in a repentant spirit. The *Irish Times* reviewer said the book would "help careful and thoughtful English readers to understand the Irish situation, and to be sympathetic. It is also a valuable reminder to Irish people of how English people can care about our legacy of hurt and bitterness without being patronising. He ends with a personal plea for healing and reconciliation to atone for what he describes as centuries of pain, and to enable the dead in Ireland to rest in peace."

Canon Frayling was able to meet with Irish President Mary Robinson and presented her with the book. He preached in Westminster Abbey on the subject. Wherever he went, he stressed the need for apology by Britain and particularly the need for the established church to take the lead. "To apologize is not to demonstrate weakness," he wrote. "Rather, it requires a particular kind of courage and statesmanship which transcends politics." He feels that there are times when representative leadership can speak of higher values. "When the head of state is a monarch, who has a particular, if symbolic, role in relation to the National Church, an apology may be held to have spiritual as well as worldly significance."

Repentance and apology alone cannot assure forgiveness or guarantee a settlement that lasts. But it is hard to think that a settlement is possible without it. This view is at the heart of Frayling's approach. He sees these steps as a supplement to the economic and political changes that may be needed and thinks that Liverpool is uniquely suited to lead the way.

Despite the agreement in 1998, in August of that year a car-bomb explosion in Omagh killed twenty-nine people and injured more than two hundred. At Christmastime that year, thousands of people walked in a candlelight procession through the town in memory of those who died. Catholics and Protestants took part in the service after churches in the town set aside their traditional carol service. In order to lift spirits in the town, a special display of Christmas decorations was put up, with the message "Peace" spelled out in large letters.

In 1997 Frayling was invited, on the strength of his book and his speeches, to attend a ceremony marking the twenty-fifth anniversary of the Bloody Sunday killings. The invitation came from the Roman Catholic community in the Creggan. Frayling carried a message from the Archbishop of Canterbury, Donald Carey, and delivered it at the mass of requiem in St. Mary's Church in the Creggan before two thousand people. It was received with prolonged applause, and he was able to shake hands with representatives of all the victims' families. He also preached on "Pardon and Peace" at five masses during that weekend. Archbishop Carey's message stated that all who are committed to Christ have a particular responsibility to work for peace: "What we share in our faith and worship is far more than that which divides us. Our common history is littered with the terrible things done in the name of culture and religion. We must relearn the language of repentance so that we can build a safe and peaceful future for the sake of our children and their children."

Canon Frayling is grateful for the fact that in 1998 Prime Minister Blair acknowledged the role of Britain in the Irish famine. He points out that Mary Robinson, speaking at the University of Coventry at the inauguration of the first school of Forgiveness and Reconciliation Studies in a British university, had said two years earlier: "Apologies do not come easily to the lips of politicians for reasons which we all understand, but with regard to the famine in my country, I cannot tell you how much an expression of regret would mean."

Frayling feels that repentance has to be constantly expressed and the stretching out of hands of friendship must be a continuing process. We need to understand the clear distinction between repentance and forgiveness: "The act of repentance, whether by a person or by an institution, invites but cannot insist on reciprocal forgiveness." People had said to him in Derry, "I am not ready to forgive your people, but you and I can be friends." Therefore, we ought never to despise or underestimate, he says, the power of small initiatives.

The rector is encouraged that in the Middle East he observed people looking at Northern Ireland as an example of peacemaking. In 1998 he was invited to lecture at the University of Bethlehem in an international conference sponsored by Sabeel, the Palestinian Institute of Liberation Theology in Jerusalem. In his lecture, reproduced in the volume *Holy Land — Hollow Jubilee,* Frayling says that Northern Ireland might seem a long way from Palestine, but it raised issues which are central to the biblical theme of Jubilee, an institution in which a king celebrated his reign by granting pardons or amnesties, forgiving debts, and freeing slaves. Jubilee is concerned with restorative justice, addressing the causes of conflict, rather than tinkering with consequences. He said, "The theme of this conference is Jubilee, the challenge of which is to live out God's justice and generosity in our lives and in the life of our nation. It is a very tough idea, the notion that justice might be restored to all who had experienced injustice, that God would set right all that had gone wrong in the life of a people."

Frayling said that at the center of the teachings of Jesus of Nazareth were forgiveness and tolerance, though these were balanced by a firm denunciation of injustice, oppression, and particularly hypocrisy. Jesus did not speak of the virtue of "peace-loving" or "peace-seeking": "Blessed are the peace-makers" was not the same thing at all. Frayling had been struck by some words of the philosopher Hannah Arendt: "The discoverer of the role of forgiveness in the realm of human affairs was Jesus of Nazareth. The fact that he made this discovery in a religious context and articulated it in religious language is no reason to take it any less seriously in a strictly secular sense."

The Britain/Northern Ireland/Ireland problem, Frayling told his audience in Jerusalem, was one of a great many conflicts around the world — just one in the alphabet of human misery from Algeria to Zaire:

> But for an Englishman it has to be the most tragic of all, for it is eight centuries old, and it concerns the very people to whom we are most closely related in the ways I described. There has to be a better way than has so far been found to set about the process of reconciliation between the peoples of our islands. Others here will already have made connections with the situations which confront them, and most obviously that which surrounds us here where we are meeting.

On July 14, 1999, a moment when the Good Friday agreement was particularly threatened, Frayling was invited to London by the Agreed Ireland Forum, a mainly Labour Party group in Parliament, to what he thought was going to be a small occasion for about a dozen people. When he arrived, he discovered to his surprise that it was a reception in Parliament to honor him for his work for reconciliation and peace. There were 27 members of Parliament present, as well as the retired Anglican Bishop of Liverpool, Lord Sheppard, and the Roman Catholic Cardinal Cahal Daly, who had flown over specially from Ireland. The Anglican Primate of Ireland, Robert Eames, sent his regrets that he could not attend, saying that "it was a richly deserved recognition."

The occasion was chaired by Kevin McNamara, who had been Shadow Northern Ireland Secretary under the previous government. He presented Frayling with a copy of George Mitchell's new book, *Making Peace,* about the work behind the scenes by this former U.S. senator to broker the Good Friday agreement. In the front of the book was an inscription from McNamara: "In recognition of the unique contribution to truth, peace and reconciliation of Canon Nicholas Frayling, Anglican Rector of Liverpool." With it was a handwritten note from British Prime Minister Tony Blair: "May the 'healing of history' become a message for the new Millennium."

Certainly, the healing of history and the contributions of people like Frayling are now needed more than ever to usher in the peace that millions long for and have voted for. At this event in the House of Commons, a new Parliamentary group, aimed at keeping the momentum going despite the difficulties, was launched. It is called "The Friends of the Good Friday Agreement."

6

Honest conversations: Americans come to grips with race

"Most of the people I'm still mad at are long dead. If I say something mean about them, Sadie will say, 'Now, Bessie, of the dead say nothing Evil.' And I try to be good.

"Sometimes I am mad at all white people, until I stop and think of the nice white people I have known in my life. OK, OK, there have been a few. I admit it. And my mother is part white, and I can't hate my own flesh and blood! There are good white people out there. Sometimes, they are hard to find, but they're out there, just look for them.

"Once in a while, God sends a good white person my way, even to this day. I think it's God's way of keeping me from becoming too mean. And when he sends a nice one to me, then I have to eat crow. And honey, crow is a tough old bird to eat, let me tell you."

— Sarah L. Delany, *Having Our Say*

Enter the chamber of the Oregon House of Representatives in the capitol building in Salem, and you are confronted by an impressive painting of Oregon settlers which dominates the chamber. It represents the forming of a provisional government in 1843 at Champoeg on the Willamette River.

If you are white, you do not note what is immediately obvious to Native Americans and African-Americans and other people of color: there are no persons like them in the painting. The population of Oregon, at the last census, was more than 90 percent white.

Open the official *Oregon Blue Book* and read the exciting history of the state. It is fascinating and well-written — but African-Americans rate only one sentence in all its twenty-seven pages.

Oregon's whiteness is not altogether accidental. In 1849, legislation was passed excluding blacks from the state, and a culture of officially sanctioned exclusion was generated whose effects are still felt. Although repealed in 1926, the act, according to an editorial in the Salem *Statesman Journal,* "provided the justification for other discriminatory laws that were enforced for nearly 100 years and helped shape racist attitudes that persist today." It was not a question of "Come and visit but don't stay," as one Oregon governor famously told tourists, but "Don't come at all."

On April 22, 1999, 150 years later, nearly 800 men and women converged on the State Capitol to face this past honestly and commit to a future of equality. In the morning the House of Representatives and Senate had passed resolutions acknowledging the state's exclusionary history, recognizing people of all races who had worked over the years for positive change, and calling for ongoing dialogue and action. The afternoon's ceremony featured the official signing of the resolutions, along with an identically worded proclamation by the governor, and the public was invited by the speaker of the House to join the legislators on the floor of the chamber. With people of all races flocking in to share the legislators' desks, crowding the side aisles, filling the galleries, and overflowing to a hearing chamber with closed circuit TV, it was, in one legislator's view, as if she were watching the people of Oregon take possession of their House for the first time.

Oregon Governor John Kitzhaber, acknowledging that it was not easy for some people to come to an event that spoke to Oregon's racist past, said, "Oregon will not be a good place for any of us to live unless it is a good place for all of us to live." Senate President Brady Adams said, "When we have injustice, we have to change. You can't have justice if you don't treat people all the same." The speaker of the House, Lynn Snodgrass, said it was a time to celebrate the heroes who had taken us away from the state's history. Some, she said, were right there in the room — men and women who had survived situations that could have crushed them. "For the part you have played in extinguishing prejudice, you are heroes," she said.

The resolution had been passed unanimously in the Senate, but seven members had voted against it in the House. "I don't believe we serve ourselves well by recalling a painful past," said one member. "What really counts is what we do today and in the future, not to engage in symbolism but in substance." There was some resentment about these votes but, as a widely published AP account reported, "There were no words of anger or blame at the ceremony, when Oregonians, of all colors and religions, packed a House chamber. Black Buffalo Soldiers dressed in traditional navy-blue uniforms and Native Americans with feather headdresses posted the flags. The House swelled with song as [African-American] former Representative Margaret Carter led the crowd in a rendition of 'The Battle Hymn of the Republic.'"

A former Oregon chief justice, Edwin Peterson, described how racist superiority had been firmly fixed in his mind by the time he was seven. In law school he had seen intellectually that this was wrong, but it took years before what he knew in his head reached his heart. "What causes racial discrimination?" he asked, and answered, "It was people like me and you." He went on, "I can learn. I can change. I have changed." But it was not easy to unlearn racist attitudes. The first step was to look at ourselves, our own awareness. Then and only then would we be able to take great steps toward a future of racial equality.

Former Senator Mark O. Hatfield, honorary co-chair of Oregon Uniting, the coalition that had initiated the event, punctured any idea people might have of "the good old days." He spoke of treaties not honored, and of the racial injustice that breeds religious intolerance and all kinds of injustice. He spoke from personal experience. Hatfield, also a former governor, said he could remember watching a Ku Klux Klan parade in Salem; he could remember exclusion practised against a neighbor; he recalled a vote in the legislature requiring every young person to attend public school, which, he pointed out, was an attempt to get rid of parochial schools; he mentioned the exclusion of Jews from society, private schools, sororities, and the upper levels of business; he told of seeing his Japanese-American friends being shipped off to internment camps, and how as a student he had to drive the great African-American singers Marian Anderson and Paul Robeson to Portland because they could not stay overnight in Salem. While serving in the U.S. Navy, too, he saw African-Americans segregated.

"Today's Oregon," he said, "is much better than the good old days because serious efforts are being made to correct past injustice." Civil rights laws had been passed in areas like public accommodation. Restitution had been made to Japanese-Americans. But, he warned, "The virus of racial injustice is highly infectious, the disease of hatred breaks out when we least expect it. And we all become victims." The unfinished agenda of justice was still each generation's responsibility. Each of us was part of one race, he concluded: the human race. This was a truth no person was too young to learn. He learned it in Sunday school class: "Red, yellow, black and white, they are all precious in his sight."

The other co-chair, Myrlie Evers-Williams, a former leader of the NAACP, said that for this legislature and government to sign on to the event and to have speakers say that they would no longer tolerate injustice, hatred, racism, was a step forward. "We must strive in Oregon," she said, "to show the rest of the nation what can be done."

An article in the Portland *Oregonian* stated, "The ceremony rung with cheers and standing ovations as leader after leader talked about a past of injustice and a future of hope." Oregon's first Hispanic legislator, State Senator Susan Castillo, was one of the rainbow of speakers. She challenged the other legislators present not to turn back the clock on the protections offered farmworkers. Japanese-American lawyer Peggy Nagae drew cheers when she looked out at the multiracial audience and said, "This is what the Oregon Legislature is going to look like."

As the Native American color guard took turns on duty with the African-American Buffalo Soldiers, Rose High Bear, from the group Wisdom of the Elders, spoke of the great cultural rebirth being enjoyed by her people. "As spirit people there is no time for anger, hatred, we do not place blame. They are not spiritual qualities and do not belong on the Indian road." She said her people were created to endure suffering. "We don't want to dishonor our ancestors who kept their ways pure. From the wisdom of the elders came great healing power." Native Americans remembered their voyages of tears, and they prayed for Europeans on their own trail of tears. "It is a great reunion," she said, "a day to reconcile, a day to heal."

Receiving the resolutions on behalf of the Oregon Historical Society, State Senator Avel Gordly said that Oregon was showing the nation the power that can come from racial healing: "It is a model of what is possible when we forgive, correct, heal and decide to move forward together."

The Coalition of Black Men had brought a busload of people to the event from the African-American community in Northeast Portland. One of those on the bus said that there was a spirit of hopefulness as they went to Salem, as if their experiences of the past were going to be vindicated and "somebody's finally telling our story."

"People were moved," he said. "It took a burden from them. You could tell people were different riding back. There was a kind of peace and fulfilment, a feeling that this was our day."

A Native American spiritual leader, Bernie Cliff, said afterward, "That was an answer to our prayers." Oregon Secretary of State Phil Keisling commented, "This may be the best thing that happens in the legislature this year."

The Champoeg settlers looked down on the proceedings in the morning and afternoon. The painting did not get mentioned in the speeches. But, reporting the event, *El Hispanic News* did so, pointing out that the absence of a single person of color was an example of the failure to recognize the whole history of Oregon, a history that included Spanish exploration, Mexicans, Chinese, Japanese, and African-Americans who were all participants in that history. "Yet it was an appropriate setting," the paper wrote, "to have the injustice of the painting serve as a backdrop to this Day of Acknowledgment."

Day of Acknowledgment

We, as Americans, have a particularly shallow connection to our history — both by our nature as easily mobile people and by the brevity of our written record. It is easy for us to deny any connection to the actions of people long dead, for it is part of our culture to believe that we can always start fresh, to start over without obligation to the past.

So it comes as something of a shock when we discover that we can't always start anew until we acknowledge what has already come to pass. We learn this in our personal relationships with our friends and our family members when we learn to talk about what causes pain between us rather than pretend it never took place. And we discover it here, this morning, in this resolution today.

In order to move forward as one people in Oregon, we must begin with acknowledging what divides us. We are, by the nature of our office, connected to the actions of a previous generation's legislature — the 1849 Oregon Territorial Legislature. From them, our power, our office descends through generation after generation to the people on the floor today. Long before we were born, the office we hold today existed — and long after we pass away from this earth, this office, this institution will exist without us. Our votes, our actions, our words are a part of something that is larger than any one of us, and our power is granted only through our elected office — an office that descends from those first members of the Oregon Territorial Legislature.

Just like today, those members of that Assembly grappled with the problems of this region. They set a budget and passed laws so that we might better live alongside of each other and prosper. Like most of our work today, their votes, their floor speeches, their mighty acts of wisdom and oration are little remembered — and, I suspect, as quickly forgotten as our day-to-day speeches and votes will be tomorrow.

Yet, one of their actions, however grounded it was in the mentality of those times, reverberates still to this day. It was a simple bill, and I suspect passed from a fundamental sense of fear for their safety — however misguided that fear might have been. It excluded — and I will use the language of that time — "Negroes and mulattoes" from the Oregon Territory for fear that they would give the Native Americans "ideas" and the white men and women found themselves to be greatly outnumbered at the time. They deliberately excluded one group of people based simply on the color of their skin, based simply on fear.

Colleagues, facing the history of race in Oregon is not pretty, nor pleasant. Nor is it taught in our schools. But mark my words, it is remembered, and it lies close to the surface waiting to be told. And while that history is filled with the loss of homes and livelihoods, of human potential never realized; it is also filled with hope and individual courage. If you listen, if you choose to hear, you will also hear the stories of individuals who triumphed over incredible odds and of leadership that stood up against the popular will.

And so it is that we come here today, this morning, to place our own mark in history, for our children, for the legislatures yet to come, for those whose names we will not ever know or faces ever see, for our time will have long passed. We say, here, this morning, with this vote, to the people we represent and to those who follow, "That we, the members of the House of Representatives of the Seventieth Legislative Assembly, recognize Oregon's discriminatory history, acknowledge people of all races and ethnic backgrounds who have worked for positive change and celebrate the progress made and encourage participation in honest interracial dialogue essential to positive social change; and be it further

Resolved, That we, the members of the House of Representatives of the Seventieth Legislative Assembly, resolve to increase public awareness of racial discrimination and work toward the full participation of racial minorities in all aspects of Oregon life, and that this Day of Acknowledgment provide focus for planning constructive dialogues and actions as we work toward a future of racial equality."

Our history, once acknowledged, is not our destiny, and from here, from this vote, we resolve to start over, to start anew and move forward with mutual respect and as one people.

State Representative Anitra Rasmussen
Oregon House of Representatives
April 22, 1999

This event in the legislature, which may have been first of its kind in the nation, was building on the work of the Richmond, Virginia-based Hope in the Cities, which is partnering with Oregon Uniting. Hope in the Cities has over the years made its twin emphases the healing of history and the holding of honest conversations between the races.

In 1993 a coalition of Richmond citizens had held a conference billed as an "honest conversation on race, reconciliation and responsibility." It featured a walk through Richmond's history in which sites of significance, good and bad, were marked. A premise was that those involved in the planning should mirror the unity they were working toward. One who helped bring that conference to birth was a Baptist minister and a participant in the civil rights struggles of the1960s, Paige Chargois. She realized that if she was really committed to building community, then she had to reach out to the people she still hated. They were the people who flew the Confederate flag.

Before the Civil War, eleven states seceded from the Union and created their own flag. Her city, Richmond, became capital of the Confederate States of America, and the Confederate flag was their banner. To Chargois, an African-American, the flag was a symbol of hatred of primarily Southern white people against black people. "Within the American psyche it suggested our annihilation or our remaining in second-class citizenship," she says. In 1997, for instance, responding to complaints by African-American leaders, the state of Maryland agreed to recall seventy-eight special license plates featuring the flag which had been issued to members of an organization, the Sons of Confederate Veterans. "Symbols are significant. Ask a Jewish person about the significance of the swastika," said Clarence Mitchell IV, an African-American member of Maryland's Legislative Black Caucus. In 1996, the Republican governor of South Carolina upset fellow conservatives when he proposed removing the Confederate flag from the last statehouse that flew it, and in 1999 two national conventions scheduled for Richmond were canceled because it still flew. In Georgia, a lawsuit was filed to force the state to remove the Confederate emblem from the state flag. The lawsuit failed, but the Eleventh Circuit Court said that because the Confederate battle flag emblem offends many Georgians, it had in their view no place in the official state flag: "We regret that the Georgia Legislature has chosen, and continues to display, as an official state symbol a battle flag emblem that divides rather than unifies the citizens of Georgia."

Flown from private houses or draped across the rear window of trucks, whenever or wherever she saw it, the flag inspired in Chargois a deep sense of hatred. "God was not content for me to live with that hatred," she says, "and yet I didn't know how to free myself from it." As she was preparing the conference dedicated to "healing the heart of America," she felt that she should move toward the things and people she hated. Her animus focused on one organization, the Daughters of the Confederacy, and those who hoisted the flag as their symbol.

In getting to know some of these white women, she came to understand that for them the flag was more a symbol of pain than of racism. One day she visited a woman who was regional vice president of the United Daughters of the Confederacy. The Confederate flag was on the woman's wall. "In order to hear a word she said to me, I had to sit with my back to the wall," remembers Chargois. The white woman began to talk about her perception of the Civil War, which was quite different from that of Chargois. "In the moments we spent together with two other friends, God said to me that I could not be free of my hatred until I acknowledged and accepted her pain. God gave me the victory. In an extraordinary way my hatred did not just diminish. It was almost instantaneously transformed."

The Baptist minister was subsequently able to bring together in dialogue both black leaders and white leaders with a Confederate heritage. That led to the executive director of the Musem of the Confederacy declaring, "The museum must become a learning center for the whole community." No longer, says Chargois, would it be merely a depository of the relics and memories of war or a repository of hatred.

Because of their skill in bringing people together in honest conversation, Chargois and Rob Corcoran, national director of Hope in the Cities, were invited by the President's Initiative on Race to help draw up *One America,* a guide to racial dialogue which was distributed widely round the country. She says, "We realized that there couldn't be any community life until we dealt honestly with the wounds of history."

The National Conference for Community and Justice, in a 1999 publication titled *Intergroup Relations in the United States,* identifies the dialogue process developed by Hope in the Cities as one of seven "promising practices" and quotes Chargois about those taking part:

> Fundamental to our way of thinking is that they take what they have learned into where they live every day. That is how real change comes about. We don't need another organization on race; we don't need another group meeting once a week into eternity. We need the same folk to get back to where they live and make that difference, so that the clerks behind the counter can be different, so that the preachers in the pulpit will be different, so that the car salesman won't give a different price to a black person than a white person.

In the spring of 1999 a fresh challenge confronted Chargois in her commitment to dealing with the wounds of history. For more than five years she had sought out any open door that would permit her to step across the threshold of racial intolerance and into the company of those who cherish the Confederate flag. The display of a portrait of Confederate hero General Robert E. Lee on Richmond's Canal Walk and subsequent demands for its removal produced a furor in the community. The war of words seemed to incite historic emotions that are more than a century old, stirring racial tensions at a level rarely experienced since the 1960s. It gave her an opportunity to reach out to both sides — Sons of the Confederate Veterans and leaders in her own African-American community — both of whom, she says, had entrenched racial positions.

"We've got to use the Canal Walk issue as a tremendous lesson," she says. "Because we keep tripping over the same racial wire. And that is ignorant and evil. The great task in front of us is to work with both sides." This she is attempting, with pain and patience, to do. By "walking in the big gap" she has come to realize that no amount of logic will work. "Hatred is not logical and racial hatred is one of the most illogical sentiments ever known to humanity." Protagonists on both sides were shouting at each other, "You just need to know the facts." They did not realize that facts can do little to sever the stubborn relationship between perceptions and emotional contempt relative to race. "We have a few hundred years of racial contempt to prove it."

Chargois defined the challenge as comforting both the bearers of the Confederate flag and those who remain contemptuous of it because it symbolizes deep-seated hatred for her own ancestors once enslaved. "All that I have had was my faith which calls me to 'a ministry of reconciliation' and a persuasion to live by absolute moral standards which include examining my motives in every area of life and within every relationship. Both have helped to usher me into a new reality: that the bearers of the Confederate flag no longer automatically represented people who wanted to annihilate me and my people; rather they simply 'waved' the symbol of their own pain which occurred in a past era they could not turn loose. The experience of 'the genuine' within me has enabled me to discover the genuine in others."

Seventy percent of the Richmond population were not significantly "bothered" by Lee going up on the floodwall. It was the thirty percent whose feelings were deep-seated and whose positions were entrenched that she sought to bring to new levels of openness and understanding. "To some degree I succeeded through five to seven hours of conversations with each side. To a greater degree I failed to be able to bring them in the same room. Both sides retreated to former positions."

It is an ongoing struggle in the community. "When will we become true builders of community instead of destroyers?" she asks. "When will we learn to nourish relationships between the racially different? The emotional capital we continue to spend on hating and ill will will soon bankrupt the very relationship within the community we seek to nourish and sustain."

In a joint article, she and Corcoran wrote in the *Times-Dispatch* that it would be highly unfortunate if the public rhetoric about General Lee and the Canal Walk were to overshadow the reality of racial healing that was taking place in the city. "Richmond has a unique opportunity to use its history, not just to bring tourist dollars but to help bring healing to the nation."

Looking back to the day that she visited the woman from the United Daughters of the Confederacy, Chargois says, "When I left her house, I didn't grasp where the new reality of having lost my hatred for the Confederate flag would take me. I could not draw from so satisfying a moment, sufficient meaning for others. I only knew that I was not the same in my feelings, my perceptions and knowledge about the human beings who had fought the Civil War and their progeny who continue to fire factual and moral salvos across the racial divide in the country."

The Civil War and the Confederate flag evoke a different memory for Richard Ruffin, whose ancestors founded Richmond. His great-great-grandfather, Edmund Ruffin, is noted in American schoolbooks because he fired the shot on Fort Sumter that marked the start of the Civil War. He was a prominent agriculturalist who served in the Virginia Legislature. At the end of the war, this owner of slave plantations and advocate of state's rights, not wanting to owe allegiance to the United States, wrapped himself in the Confederate flag and ended his life with a bullet.

Ruffin had wondered for a long time how to evaluate his ancestor. He had been brought up on stories of his ancestor's passion to save the South's rural economy and his struggle for slavery and secession. And, despite misgivings about his purposes, he absorbed a certain pride in Edmund Ruffin's agricultural innovations and radical politics. It was only comparatively recently that he had realized that his ancestor's life had indirectly touched his own, and that his legacy in subtle ways shaped his own relationships with African-Americans.

To understand the legacy of the Civil War, Ruffin believes, you have to recognize that the defeat of the South was felt as a deep humiliation, leaving a residue of resentment, insecurity, and anger. One effect was that white Southerners interpreted their experience in respect to the North, rather than to the blacks. It was seen as a humiliation; Southerners were the victims, and their enemies were the villains.

To judge from his diaries and Ruffin family lore, Edmund Ruffin was not conscious of the evil of slavery or of the havoc it wreaked in the lives of millions of Africans and their descendants. Not surprisingly, in stories passed down in families like this, black Americans hardly ever figured. Their reality was ignored, their true feelings denied. "Such blindness was in some measure bequeathed to subsequent generations," says Ruffin, "so that many in my generation still have little capacity to feel the reality of what life was for the bonded Americans, or for their descendants today."

In the Richmond *Times-Dispatch* in 1993, Ruffin wrote of a second and perhaps more persistent legacy: a minimalist view of the potential of African-Americans. "Those who saw blacks as property did little to pass on to their children a positive idea of what blacks could contribute to American thought, politics, business and culture." People like himself, he said, needed to recognize and appreciate the extraordinary contributions already made by African-Americans and to find fresh vision for their future role. Black Americans needed to see whites ending the denial that had blinded them.

After describing his history and the legacies of denial and low expectations for his African-American brothers and sisters which it had bequeathed to his generation, Ruffin wrote that he had repented of these things and was seeking personally the moral and spiritual rearmament that the country needed. "Only then," he said, "can we together complete the American experiment and make America whole."

Another person working with Hope in the Cities is Joe Carter, an African-American singer from Minnesota, and a great-nephew of the educator Mary McLeod Bethune. Carter has known racial discrimination and police harassment, but to him forgiveness is a choice which liberates him and sets in motion the possibility of change in others. He uses his talent to bring the world in song and story the pain and struggle of his people and the message of forgiveness. "If I have hate for another human being," he says, "I am not free."

On one occasion, the six-foot four-inch singer was accosted by a much smaller white man on a Las Vegas street. The man, as

Carter puts it, "used the N-word." Carter's immediate thought was, "This man has a problem. He also must be a masochist to pick on the biggest black man around." Carter smiled and said, "Good morning, you look a bit under the weather this morning. I hope you'll feel better as the day goes by." As he looked back he saw the man scratching his head, bewildered, embarrassed, and disarmed. To Carter it was a demonstration of his belief that "there can be a right response to a wrong action."

In 1999 Carter undertook a thirty-seven-city tour presenting his music and convictions to thousands of all-white communities in rural America. "After the concert," he says, "I try to shake every hand and look into the faces of the people. For most I am the only black person they have ever come in touch with. I sense the awful responsibility laid upon me to share a message which encourages the best in people and helps to tear down walls of prejudice."

Carter says that people do not respond to being beaten over the head for their shortcomings. "When I deal with the pain and tragedy of racism I also talk about the good people who risked everything to help slaves escape on the Underground Railroad and those multitudes who gave their lives for the cause of freedom in the bloody Civil War." He talks about dealing with his own prejudices, and jokes about how sure he was at one point in his life that he was above all that and had none of his own but found that he had apparently borrowed a few. "As the light of honest self-examination shines, it is like peeling back the layers of an onion: there always seems to be another layer yet to be removed."

People listen to Joe Carter. But how do you talk to someone who won't listen to you, and how do you love someone who won't let you love them? That was the challenge addressed by Richard Brown some years earlier.

In 1954, as a result of the Supreme Court decision in the case of *Brown* (no relation to Richard Brown) *v. Board of Education,* all American schools were required to be desegregated. Professor Brown was teaching at Bluefield State College in West Virginia. There was a delay in the courts' enforcing this change, but by the late 1960s, as as a result of that ruling, Bluefield State — which up to that point had been an all-black college — became predominantly white, both in its faculty and in its student body. Brown, who was then dean, found himself number two to a white president. Most staff and students accepted the position, except for three white professors who made life hell for Brown. This was a particularly difficult period also because of the campus turbulence in reaction to the Vietnam War.

As dean, Brown had committed himself to a policy of caring for everyone equally as best he could, but, as he said, these folks would not let him love them. And after a while he began to hate them passionately. One morning, taking time for quiet reflection, he had the thought: "You can't always decide how you feel about people but you can decide how you treat them. Treat them as though they were your best friends, so that anyone looking on would think they were your brothers."

"I certainly didn't feel that way," he says. "But at least I could try."

For some time Brown worked on these inner guidelines. One of the white men was Brown's deputy in math and chemistry. After a few months he came to Brown and said, "I notice you have been very busy of late so I have worked out the schedule for math and chemistry for the next semester." The men began to talk and remained friends until Brown's death. Then, a little later, a second formerly inimical professor came to him and told him that one of his family was in trouble and that Brown was the only person he felt he could talk to about it. The third man took a little longer, but by the end of the year he too had reconciled with Brown. Together they worked to make Bluefield State a pattern of voluntary desegregation. For this, Brown was honored by his city council.

In 1995 an event took place in the United States that was neither as dramatic nor as difficult as the decision made by the Dutch Reformed Church synod in South Africa to apologize for having provided religious justification for apartheid. But it was nevertheless an important decision for U.S. society and drew headlines across the country.

This was the formal apology by the overwhelmingly white Southern Baptist Convention (SBC) for having condoned racism throughout much of its history. The SBC was formed in 1845 when Southern Baptists disagreed with Northern Baptists about slave-holding, and broke away rather than give up their slaves. It is the largest Protestant denomination in the United States, with nearly sixteen million members in 39,910 churches, of which about 1,800 are predominantly African-American.

The apology, adopted at the SBC's annual meeting in Atlanta, came in a strongly worded resolution repudiating "historic acts of evil such as slavery" and asking for forgiveness. The messengers, as Baptist delegates are called, said, "We apologize to all African-Americans for condoning or perpetuating individual and systemic racism in our lifetime, and we genuinely repent of racism of which we have been guilty, whether consciously or unconsciously." The vote in favor of the resolution received a standing ovation from 20,000 members at the meeting. Referring to the resolution in his closing address to the SBC, Billy Graham said, "I want to say, thank God. That'll help my ministry all over the world."

Gary Frost, second vice president of the SBC, said, "On behalf of my black brothers and sisters we accept your apology. We pray that the genuineness of your repentance will be reflected in your attitudes and in your actions." Another African-American Southern Baptist minister, George McCalep, answered critics of the resolution who saw the action as motivated by a desire to recruit members more widely. "God's spirit went before the resolution," he said. "Repentant hearts brought it. The resolution is evidence of what God has already worked in the hearts of men and women. Racism is the number one sin in America. When the largest Protestant body makes a statement against the undergirding of sin in America, it's significant."

An editorial in the St. Louis *Post-Dispatch* commented, "The willingness to admit — and apologize for — the sins of the past can be a transforming experience because it can force one to look at the present and future with a more honest eye." And the *Atlanta Journal* editorialized, "The apology and acceptance of same, is a foundation on which to build a future racial relationship of openness and honesty." Carl T. Rowan, nationally syndicated African-American columnist of the Chicago *Sun-Times,* in an open letter to the president of SBC, wrote, "I take your resolution as a genuine expression of a godliness that can meet the needs of America's very troubled time. It will take a Christ-like miracle to move this America away from paranoid bigotry, mindless meanness, grotesque greed and the embrace of 1995-type slavery. But if the preachings of Jesus that one good person can make a difference are valid, I shall not doubt that more than 15 million newly dedicated Southern Baptists can make a nation-saving difference."

On October 9, 1990, the attorney general of the United States knelt at the feet of a wheelchair-bound, 107-year-old Japanese-American, Mamoru Eto, and presented him with a check for $20,000 and an apology from the nation. "By finally admitting a wrong," said Dick Thornburgh, "a nation does not destroy its integrity but, rather, reinforces the sincerity of its commitment to the Constitution and hence to its people."

Eto was one of the 120,000 Americans of Japanese ancestry, two-thirds of them born in the United States, who at a time of anti-Japanese hysteria after the attack on Pearl Harbor were forcibly relocated and interned in what the Japanese American Citizens League called "concentration camps." Eto was, at the time, minister of the First Nazarene Japanese Church in Pasadena. "They were not death camps," as *Los Angeles Times* writer Betty Cuniberti put it, "but freedom, pride, and dreams died a thousand times in California, in Colorado, in Arizona, and in Wyoming, in the sprawling makeshift camps to which Japanese Americans were herded."

Congress authorized the payment of $1.25 billion in reparations for what some lawmakers describe as "this American shame." The money was given to about 65,000 people: surviving internees or their descendants.

The mass relocation in 1943 followed Executive Order 9066, signed by President Franklin D. Roosevelt, moving persons of Japanese ancestry away from the West Coast because of "military necessity," so it was appropriate that accompanying each check was a statement from President George Bush: "We can never fully right the wrongs of the past. But we can take a clear stand for justice and recognize that serious injustices were done to Japanese Americans during World War II."

Robert T. Matsui, a U.S. congressman from Sacramento, spent the first few years of his life in a California camp. About the same time, his wife, Doris, was born in a camp in Colorado. Matsui was a sponsor of the Civil Liberties Act, which authorizes the apology and the restitution, along with another California representative, Norman Y. Mineta, who was interned as a ten-year-old in Wyoming, and senators Daniel Inouye and Spark Matsunaga. Matsui saw the outcome as a major victory, not only for those who were interned but also for Congress and the country, and an end to an "arduous national march toward redemption." He did not receive any money; he waived that right so that he could vote for the bill on the floor of the House.

Twenty thousand dollars per person represented a small fraction of the funds lost by Japanese-Americans through relocation or the replacement of lost property or livelihood. However, as one Japanese-American said in a television interview, he was grateful for the money, but what meant most was the apology.

What had hurt the Japanese community was the impugning of their loyalty as Americans and the persecution they suffered because of their race. Many Japanese-Americans were serving in the U.S. forces while their families were forced to live in camps. Japanese-American volunteers fought in the famous 100th Infantry Battalion and in the 442nd Regimental Combat Team, which had the highest casualty rate and most decorations of any unit of its size in all U.S. military history.

Speaking at the moving ceremony in the Justice Department, Attorney General Thornburgh said, "I am not unmindful of the historic role this Department of Justice played in the internment. It is somehow entirely fitting that it is here we now celebrate redress." Representatives Matsui and Mineta embraced, in tears, as the audience in the Great Hall sang "God Bless America." Mineta said, "Americans of Japanese ancestry now know in their hearts that the letter and the spirit of our Constitution holds true for them."

Spencer Perkins, an African-American, co-author with Chris Rice, a white man, of *More Than Equals,* and co-leader with him of Reconcilers Fellowship, a movement among Christians for racial reconciliation, died in 1994 at age forty-four. In his last public statement, quoted in *Christianity Today* (July 13, 1998), he said that the United States was at an impasse over race because of the absence of forgiveness:

Although we must continue to speak on behalf of those who are oppressed and warn oppressors, my willingness to forgive them is not dependent on how they respond. Being able to extend grace and to forgive people sets us free. We no longer need to spend precious emotional energy thinking about the day oppressors will get what they deserve.

What I am learning about grace lifts a weight from my shoulders, which is nothing short of invigorating.When we can forgive and accept those who refuse to listen to God's command to do justice, it allows them to hear God's judgment without feeling a personal judgment from us. Which, in the end gives our message more integrity. The ability to give grace while preaching justice makes our witness even more effective.

7

When the guns fall silent: Turning enemies into friends

"Father forgive"

— Inscription at Coventry Cathedral

"Sleep in peace. We will not make the same mistake again."

— Inscription at Hiroshima Memorial

During the 1898 Battle of Santiago, the sailors on board the battleship USS *Texas* cheered as the Spanish ship *Viscaya* was sunk. Their captain, John Woodward Philip, tried to restrain them: "Don't cheer, boys, the poor devils are dying." In the heat of battle, compassion is naturally often missing. Forgiveness is not uppermost in many people's minds.

But when the war is over, there is an opportunity for generosity. At the Japanese surrender at the end of World War II, in a ceremony on board the USS *Missouri*, General Douglas MacArthur spoke in a way that deeply impressed the Japanese. He said:

The issues, involving divergent ideals and ideologies, have been determined on the battlefields of the world and hence are not for our discussion or our debate. Nor is it for us here to meet ... in a spirit of distrust, malice or hatred. But rather it is for us, both victors and vanquished, to rise to that higher dignity which alone benefits the sacred purpose we are about to serve.... It is the hope of all mankind that from this solemn occasion a better world shall emerge out of the blood and carnage of the past, a world founded upon faith and understanding, a world dedicated to the dignity of man and the fulfillment of his most cherished wish for freedom, tolerance and justice.

The South African writer Laurens van der Post, who was a prisoner of war of the Japanese, spoke for many when he said, "Our way has always been to try and make friends of the enemy when the guns fall silent." Sadly, however, that is not always the case. In this chapter, there are stories of forgiveness after war from New Zealand, Poland, Laos, Argentina, Ethiopia, Somalia, and Vietnam.

Germany's Field Marshal Erwin Rommel once said, "Give me the Maori battalion and I will conquer the world." He was speaking of the courage of the World War II Allied army unit drawn from the native people of New Zealand. Perhaps the most famous battle in which the Maori battalion participated was at Monte Cassino in Italy. The chaplain to the battalion, whose bravery in the battle won him Britain's Military Cross, was Canon Wi Te Tau Huata, later chaplain to the Maori queen. The citation spoke of his indifference to fire as he brought in the wounded.

Son and grandson of Anglican priests, Canon Huata believed his people were meant to be peacemakers in the Pacific. In his work to bring New Zealand's Maori and Pakeha (European) communities together, he drew on his experience in finding an answer to what he called "the cancer of bitterness" — his hatred of Germans and his prejudice against Catholics.

Twenty-five years after the war, on his way to a conference center in Switzerland, Huata's plane flew over Monte Cassino and the pilot, unaware of its significance to his passenger, pointed it out below. For Huata it revived painful memories. As chaplain he had buried the many Maori casualties of the battle.

At the conference, the New Zealand party was welcomed by a German woman, Fulvia Spoerri, who in the course of describing how the center operated, said, "I am a German; many of my generation call themselves Europeans. We are ashamed of the cost paid by your countries on the other side of the world for our actions in the second World War. We don't ask you to forget; we do ask your forgiveness."

Canon Huata stormed out of the meeting. He said to a friend shortly afterward that it was one of the worst moments of his life: "I was reminded of all the friends I buried in Italy and of my prayer during those days, 'God destroy Hitler and wipe the Germans off the face of the earth.'"

The friend asked, "What do you feel about it?"

"I need to apologize to that woman," said Huata. "I have been a priest all these years and I have carried this hate in my heart." He recalled that his wife had asked him before they came, "What are going to do when you meet Germans?" His reply was that he would wait until it happened.

At that point Spoerri walked by, and so Huata stopped her, apologized, and asked her forgiveness.

The next morning he spoke at a session of the conference and repeated his apology for all the Germans present and spoke of the need for reconciliation within families and nations. Unknown to him, there were officers present from the German Afrika Korps, and they came up to shake his hand.

The interaction with Germans at the conference affected his whole life. He said that unity with his family and unity with former enemies followed when he put right what he had done wrong. "While I held bitterness I was blind to the needs of our own family." He decided to shed his bitterness about his eldest son's marrying a Catholic. "I never forgave him until I saw that 'love your neighbor' includes those not in the Anglican Church!"

At the conference Huata made friends with the nephew of General Westphal, Rommel's successor as commander of the

Afrika Korps. As a result, the Maori Battalion was sent an invitation to the next Afrika Korps reunion. Huata read the invitation to veterans assembled at a cathedral service before their own reunion in New Zealand. He told them the story of what had happened to him.

Twenty-six Maoris responded — and were given a tumultuous reception by the seven thousand Afrika Korps veterans. Canon Huata was seated beside Frau Rommel and her son, Manfred, and was asked to speak. "This is a time for brotherhood," he said. "A time for reconciliation. A time for forgiveness. A time for cleansing. We cannot spell 'forgiving' without spelling 'giving.' We cannot spell 'brothers' without 'others.' We cannot spell 'communion' without 'union.'"

General Westphal responded, "Your greatness is not only in battle but also in your hearts by accepting our invitation of goodwill."

Huata liked to quote the words of another Afrika Korps veteran when he saw Huata's broad girth: "We must have been lousy shots to miss you."

The report of the visit to Germany in New Zealand's *Waikato Times* said, "Canon Huata has continually advocated that no person can have hate in their soul and Christ too. He has made this message plain to both Maori and Pakeha. It seems to have made its mark in other parts of the world."

Olgierd and Aniela Stepan, Poles now living in England, see the broad sweep of forgiveness in its powerful effect on their native country and its depth in a fundamental experience that has transformed their own lives. To any list of examples of national reconciliation through forgiveness they would add that of the Polish bishops addressing the German nation in 1965 and asking, "after all the horrendous activities of the Nazi occupation," to "forgive and forget" the past and move on, as a new creation, toward the future with and in Jesus. The Polish bishops stated, "In this very Christian and at the same time very human spirit, we extend our hands to you forgiving and asking forgiveness." The German bishops responded "with emotion and joy."

The Stepans called it "a tremendous act of courage," with many bishops, priests, and Catholics being castigated by the Communist regime as "pro-German." It removed a major political argument for Soviet protection against "vengeful Germans." It liberated the Roman Catholic Church in Poland to play a role in the international scene and in some measure, they say, paved the way for the election of Cardinal Wojtyla to the papal throne. "Yes, what a great and liberating power is true forgiveness."

Olgierd Stepan, a leading Polish Catholic layman in Britain, says that in his work with the European Forum of Catholic Laity Councils he is in regular dialogue with Germans. The Forum has established some pragmatic rules for their encounters which promote mutual understanding and openness. "Honesty is fundamental and so is respect for the other person's views," he says.

That the Stepans should be so open to meeting with Germans cannot be taken for granted, considering their harrowing adventures during World War II. They grew up in western Ukraine when it was Polish. They suffered at the hands of both Germans and Russians. Aniela, then fifteen, remembers the time vividly: "The German planes would use us as live target practice, shooting at people and cows in the fields. Cities were bombed regularly and civilian casualties were huge." Shortly after Hitler invaded Poland from the west, the Soviet army in September moved in from the east.

The KGB searched their house, announced that they were to be deported for twenty-five years, took them to the station, and put them in a cattle truck. They were being taken as forced labor to northern Russia. On the three-week journey, their only food was bread every second day and whatever they had managed to bring. Aniela remembers that on three occasions they were given hot soup.

Over the next six months, several hundred trains carried over 1.5 million Poles, about a tenth of the country's population, into the Soviet Union. "We were so much luckier than Aniela," says Olgierd. "By then it was already spring." Four months earlier his father, an architect, had been arrested by the KGB. Olgierd never saw him again; he died in a Soviet prison.

The following year the Germans invaded the Soviet Union, and Aniela headed south to join those who were forming a new Polish army. Judged too weak to enlist, she was eventually sent to a school in Palestine. On Easter Day of 1945, she met Olgierd at the American University in Beirut, and the next year they were married. In 1950 they decided to settle in London.

Wanting to leave the past behind, the Stepans plunged into life in Britain. But in 1956, when Soviet tanks crushed the Hungarian uprising, Olgierd was surprised by the depth of his emotion. He realized that the moment in history when he was born and the language learned from his mother were gifts from God. "I realized I had to respect God's choices and live not as an escapist, but with my culture and my nation." He felt he was being called to be "a voice for those who are downtrodden and betrayed." The experience led to his involvement with the Polish Institute of Catholic Action, of which he was chairman from 1968 to 1986.

Returning to Poland for the first time since her childhood, Aniela was urged by a priest to visit Auschwitz, where tens of thousands of her countrymen and women had died. Aniela had never hated the Russians or the Ukrainians, despite her suffering. She had seen how much they, too, had suffered under Stalin. But her hatred of the Germans had stayed with her. She resisted the suggestion, frightened of the evil that the concentration camp represented. But the priest insisted. In *Rediscovering Freedom,* her experience is described:

> After so many years, it still terrified me. The priest took me to the wall of death. We saw the mountain of discarded shoes that still remain there, the mountain of shaven hair. Suddenly I saw the whole history. I felt I had to get out. Yet I couldn't move. I was paralyzed. Opposite the wall of death stands a huge cross where public hangings used to take place. I turned and saw it. I felt, like Christ, completely broken. I was so frightened of the hatred of the Germans that was in me. They had for me been the worst symbol of evil. It had been organized on a mass scale that was unbelievable.

I cried out, "My God, my God, help me!" Suddenly I saw the outstretched arms of Christ. I heard his words, "Father, forgive them for they know not what they are doing." The words were repeated, and then, "I died for them. I died for them." For me it was the greatest victory — not mine but his. From being completely beaten I became a totally new person. At that moment, when I knew I was reborn, the gratitude I felt to God was overwhelming. But what is more important is that I no longer hate. Now I pray for the Germans each day

Olgierd Stepan believes that a grace of the same order, though on a far wider scale than that experienced by his wife, is needed in eastern and central Europe now that the lid of totalitarianism has been lifted and extreme nationalistic hatred released once more.

The Stepans say that "a person is at his or her fullest when offering forgiveness; then we are most truly 'in his image.'" As Catholics, they believe that confession to a priest, acting *"in persona Christi,"* is most helpful. But the act of forgiveness has a dual effect of freeing the injurer from his guilt and remorse, and freeing the injured from negative feelings toward that person, and quite often toward himself. "It is a profoundly liberating experience, leaving the 'land of slavery' to the Promised land of loving. It is also a costly experience. It links one with the Atonement of Jesus on the Cross and participates in his suffering and victory."

Tianethone Chantharasy and his wife, Viengxay, live in Australia, the country to which he was once the Laotian chargé d'affaires. Tianethone was ambassador to India in 1970 and afterward secretary of state for foreign affairs in the last coalition government in his country before the Communists took over in 1975. In exile, he became secretary general of the United Lao National Liberation Front. The wellbeing of the half-million Laotian refugees scattered throughout the world is a principal concern. The Chantharasys have personally taken responsibility to collect medicines and clothes for many refugees in camps. In Sydney the family is also active in the community. Tianethone told his local newspaper, "We should all plant trees that we never sit under in life. Volunteer work is wonderful."

The struggle for freedom for him began in the 1940s, when he was enrolled as a young man in his country's army of national liberation, struggling to oust the French colonial government. The Chantharasys could with good reason hate the French, the Japanese, the Americans, the Communists, and especially the North Vietnamese Communists, who occupied Laos, killed thousands of Laotians in concentration camps, and tried to create a new race through forced marriages between Vietnamese and Laotians. They are still passionate about freeing their country from foreign domination, but they have chosen to break what they call "the chain of hate." Tianethone asks, "If you have hatred against your brother, how can you liberate your country?"

In an essay, "Prospects of National Reconciliation in Laos," which he wrote in 1995 on behalf of leaders of the Laotian community in Australia, Chantharasy says that Laos has been cursed with a vicious cycle of hatred and revenge. In order to succeed, an attempt at national reconciliation needs a new dimension: national forgiveness. "The chain of hate in the hearts of leaders and educated Laotians must first be broken as part of any attempt to tackle the problems facing the nation."

He believes that no Laotian can forget, but they can forgive; the list of dangers of nonforgiveness is long. One of them is that people remain prisoners of the past, harboring constant collective memories of resentment and hate which are capable of triggering new armed conflicts. The path of reconciliation through forgiveness among Laotian political leaders is untried and will be arduous. "But with strong and courageous political will and a clear vision from both sides, the chain of hatred and revenge will be broken."

The present Communist regime in Laos, he says, has an agreement with Vietnam tying their country to Vietnam militarily, politically, economically, and culturally. It is in essence a "province" of its neighbor. But he takes hope from the fact that Laos was admitted to ASEAN (the Association of South East Asian Nations) in 1997, and ASEAN calls for the creation of open societies in each of its member states by the year 2002. He and other Laotian expatriates are making every effort to see that the National Assembly elections due that year are openly contested and free and fair. After the elections, he would like to see a general amnesty for and liberation of all prisoners both of the left and right, and a suppression of pejorative distinctions between the former regime and the present one. This would create a new situation "conducive to genuine collective forgiveness and national reconciliation."

The Chantharasys' passion to win back their country to freedom and democracy is matched by their desire to create a Laotian society in the future that would be impervious to takeover. "We must have the insight to see beyond the liberation of Laos," Tianethone tells his fellow countrymen and women, "because we have seen in many other countries that after liberation there has been a change of power but the bloodshed continues. We need to start on a new basis and build trust, confidence, love, and respect for different tribes and ethnic minorities."

In this approach they build on their commitment to Buddhism, in which, he believes, lies "the greatest hope" for his country. "We need to neutralize the power of hatred and hold collective ceremonies of prayer and forgiveness in all Laotian pagodas around the world. Forgiveness is not a panacea to all the problems, but will open the opportunity to bring real peace and prosperity to Laos."

The Chantharasys are alive today because of their generous approach to all and their effort to reach out even to those who disagree with them. While Tianethone was in the coalition government, he and Viengxay were working to lay moral foundations for their society. A young leftist militant observed them and was attracted by what he felt was a universal approach. One day in May 1975, he went to a cell meeting and discovered that Chantharasy as a nationalist minister in the government was on the list for arrest that night. He rushed to the Chantharasy home and persuaded them to leave. The Chantharasys packed a few belongings, got the prime minister's permission to go, left by the back door, and crossed the Mekong River into Thailand. Fifteen minutes later, Pathet Lao soldiers arrived at their house to arrest them.

In 1998 President Carlos Menem of Argentina laid a wreath in Britain in honor of British soldiers who died in the Falklands/Malvinas War, and in 1999 Prince Charles made a similar gesture of reconciliation in Argentina. Charles also shook hands with veterans of the war in Buenos Aires. At the highest level, the effort is being made to build bridges. It is not always easy. President Menem was criticized for his expression of regret because it might be interpreted as an apology, and Prince Charles came under attack for stepping into politics when he expressed a hope that the people of the islands and the Argentinians might establish a good relationship.

Bridges are also being built at the level of the fighting soldier. Horacio Benitez, a young Argentinian conscript, was left for dead on the Falklands/Malvinas battlefield. Wrapped in a blanket, with a bullet in his skull, he was lying with a pile of corpses when a British sergeant saw his eyes blink. He took him to a medical crew who saved his life.

"I was a soldier in the front line of battle," he says, "I was given the last rites three times. I survived but I felt a strong hatred. I had lost many friends. I really regret this killing of people. But there is still something we can do to help change the world so that this may never happen again." At a meeting in Buenos Aires after the war he asked some British present for forgiveness from the families left without fathers and sons.

On a visit to London, Benitez asked if he could meet the commander of the British parachute regiment against whom he had fought. He had traumatic memories of emptying two machine-gun rounds into advancing British soldiers. Asked by a reporter from the Guardian about his request, he said, "You ask yourself how many fathers you have killed. And you ask yourself 'why.'" He wanted to seek out those in the British military to whom he could express his regret.

His British hosts happened to know the whereabouts of the British commander, Lieutenant Colonel Chris Keeble, who agreed to meet his former foe. The atmosphere was charged with emotion as they met. They embraced. Benitez broke into tears. He says, "It was so emotional I couldn't speak. I think this was the moment the war really ended for me. It was the strangest feeling. He seemed like an old, very deep friend."

Colonel Keeble says that he listened patiently for two hours to Benitez's search for forgiveness. Then he asked the Argentinian soldier what it would be like in his country if the war had not been fought. After hearing a depressing picture of military dictatorship, he suggested to Benitez that they were "both on the same side, the side of good versus evil." "It was from this realization that he was freed from his guilt," says Keeble. "It was the idea of goodness that created forgiveness and not my action."

The British officer believes that the nature of war is for combatants to "suffer" together on a battlefield in order that some greater injustice may be remedied. "Thus the idea of 'passion,' of 'suffering,' is intrinsic to forgiveness," he says. "Combatants create the bridge for others to find the good."

In the Falklands battle, Keeble, then a major, found himself in charge of his paratroop battalion when they were attacking Goose Green after his commanding officer was shot dead. It was bitterly cold; his men had been fighting for forty hours, and one in six of the battalion had been either injured or killed. They were in a perilous position, and he had the responsibility to say what should be done. He knelt in the gorse and said a prayer that he carried with him: "Father, I abandon myself to you. Do with me as you will. Whatever you may do with me I thank you, provided your will is fulfilled in me. I ask for nothing more."

The result was a real transformation, he says. Instead of feeling frightened and confused, he felt joyful and had what he calls immense clarity about what to do. He told his men that at first light he would walk across the battlefield and invite the Argentinians to surrender. The men were astounded. "We were a unit that was designed to bring violence to produce a solution, and I was offering one that was completely the reverse. "

But that is exactly what he did, accompanied by his artillery officer and a BBC journalist. Later, he discovered they had walked through a minefield. He appealed to the Argentinians' common Catholic faith to put an end to the bloodshed. By midday, the Argentinians agreed to surrender with dignity. They held a formal parade, sang their national anthem, and laid down their arms. "I was offering them something they wanted," Keeble says, "but I could not have known that." The size of the Argentine garrison amazed the British: 1,500 troops surrendered to 450 British paratroopers.

Michael Smith, describing this event in the magazine *For a Change,* commented, "The surrender saved many lives and set the tone for the rest of the war." Three weeks later, Keeble's troops were the first into Port Stanley for the final surrender.

Keeble and Benitez both found the direction of their lives changed by the war. Both decided to use their lives for others. Keeble works with a development group where he "can contribute to other people's growth" and Benitez, now a businessman, initiated a cooperative for war veterans. Keeble hopes one day he and Benitez will be able to revisit the Falklands together. "After all," he says, "we are on the same side."

Mammo Wudneh is president of the Ethiopian Writers Union and a respected historian with more than forty books in print. He has been working to resolve tension and end fighting between Ethiopia and Eritrea. He told a 1998 conference in Europe that he was concerned that both sides were purchasing expensive weapons from eastern Europe, Asia, and maybe, he said, western Europe as well. He feared that the conflict could widen and affect the neighboring countries, endangering stability in the Horn of Africa:

> It is very unfortunate that as we are gathered here to find the best ways for peace, two countries which are in many ways sisters are immersed in the tension of conflict with each other. When will the human person learn that violence is not the answer and never will be? Are not so many human lives which may easily be lost in war more important than the border? Armed conflict is an evil potential that could leave countless people killed, maimed, orphaned and homeless.

Wudneh appealed to the two countries — and indeed, all countries in conflict — to stop all forms of hostility and violence. He urged those present to enlist their countries in this peace-building effort. Already two months earlier Wudneh had gathered the different religious leaders of his country, from the Christian, Muslim, and other faith communities, for an interfaith peace meeting chaired by the patriarch of the Ethiopian Orthodox Church. He reported that a permanent committee composed of these leaders has been established and was active.

In taking these initiatives and launching an appeal to the world, Wudneh was building on earlier experiences in his own life. During World War II, his parents and relatives were killed when the Italian Fascist Air Force bombed his village. Thirty years later, he met an old man who proudly told him that he was a pilot at the time of the Italian occupation of Ethiopia and that he had bombarded Wudneh's village. Wudneh says that he shivered and became furious and went to his room to get a pistol so he could take his revenge. "Yet, my conscience forced me to think twice," he says. "I then begged God to show me the right direction and help to guide me. The answer came, if I killed the Italian Fascist, would my parents and relatives be alive? At a time when people all over the world forgive the past wrongdoing and live in peace with tolerance, if I killed an old man, does this not mean repeating the same mistake committed by Mussolini?"

The Ethiopian writer thought it over. The next day he went back to the bar where he had met the pilot and told him his story. "He was shocked, he was trembling thinking I was going to take revenge on him. I told him that I forgive him. 'I am sorry, sorry, please forgive me,' he replied," and they embraced. "I also kissed him," says Wudneh.

Wudneh is a courageous man. During the reign of Emperor Haile Selassie, he spoke against policies he felt were wrong. During the civil war between Ethiopia and Eritrea, he risked his life for Ethiopian-Eritrean relations. And in 1987, when dictator Mengistu Haile Mariam invited several heads of African states to attend his party congress, Wudneh got up and opposed him. As the writer resumed his seat, the president of Zambia, Kenneth Kaunda, rose to his feet and said, "This man speaks in the true spirit of pan-Africanism and for our future generations."

Ahmed Hussen Egal from Somalia told the International Forum of the Labour Party in Copenhagen in 1998 that he was part of "a network of Somalis who fight for reconciliation." His great-grandfather had been a chief. When Egal was twenty-five, the dictator arrested him and his whole family, even though they belonged to the same clan as the dictator. Egal was released after a year but had lost all his civil rights and so fled to Ethiopia. In 1978 he was among those who formed the first armed opposition group, calling itself the "Democratic Front for the Salvation of Somalia."

"Some of us intellectuals later criticized our guerrilla leaders," Egal said in Copenhagen. "For this I spent another year in jail, this time an Ethiopian one. This made me very bitter." When he was released he realized that they would never reach their aims by armed means, and he asked for asylum in Sweden. On a study course in Swedish, he met another refugee who had been the leader of the farmer's Solidarity movement in Poland; from this man he learned that change had to start with himself. "Earlier I had thought mostly of how others needed to be different."

In 1993 when the war and starvation was at its worst, Egal was given the opportunity to go to Somalia with a Swedish aid organization. The trip gave him an opportunity to look up his former guerrilla leader and ask him for forgiveness for his bitterness and hatred. "I told him that I had wanted to kill him if I had got the chance. But now I am free from my hate. When he gradually understood what I meant, he forgave me. Then I said to him that now both of us must forgive our worst enemy — General Aideed."

The guerrilla leader replied, "Now, Ahmed, you are going too far. That man is to blame for the thousands of orphans we have. They would never forgive me if I made peace with him."

Egal replied, "If we do not make peace, many more children will be orphans and they will blame us."

Four weeks later, Egal was surprised to hear on the BBC Somali newscast that this man had traveled with some of his people to Mogadishu, and that on the airfield he became reconciled with

Aideed. "I do not know if it was our conversation that lay behind it. But I am very grateful that it happened. It is extremely important for the future of Somalia that my guerrilla leader started to understand what forgiveness and reconciliation is all about because he is one of the five men who have been chosen by the different factions to lead the country towards a transitional government."

A Vietnam war veteran describes how he held in his hands the heart that had just been blown through his buddy's back. Another American of the same age tells of blowing off his toes to avoid being drafted to Vietnam. Each, for the first time, begins to understand the pain of the other. They are two sides of a searing experience which still divides Americans and which few are ready to talk about together.

"You have to go through these painful experiences before you can come out of them," says Jack Estes. He and his wife, Colleen O'Callaghan, organized the event at Portland State University at which this frank exchange took place. Their aim was to help heal the trauma of a war that is measured in the United States alone by 58,000 killed, 300,000 wounded, and more than 60,000 veterans who have since killed themselves. Portland State University was the scene of virulent anti-war demonstrations in 1970.

"My family knows about pain," says Estes, who was a Marine in Vietnam and wrote a memoir of the war, *A Field of Innocence*. "They have seen it in my face and heard it in my voice and lived it in a dozen different ways." While he was fighting in Vietnam, Colleen, not then his wife, was participating in anti-war rallies in Oregon. She disagrees with his belief that it was a legitimate war and that anti-war demonstrations prolonged the fighting. It is perhaps their willingness to work through their own differences that enables them to win the trust of those on both sides.

"War is a community effort," says Colleen, "and healing from war is a community effort. We need communications between veterans, draft-dodgers, anti-war demonstrators and those oblivious."

After returning from his service in Vietnam, Jack Estes was consumed by nightmares. "The war was with me, seared in my memory and pounding at my sensibility," he says. Finally, at

Colleen's urging he went back to Vietnam in 1993 with their family. They brought along medical supplies, books, and toys, and wandered around giving them away.

In March 1969, Estes had been with a platoon that was overrun by the Viet Cong. Most were killed or wounded. His life was saved by Hien, a villager. For twenty-five years Jack had thought about Hien. On that first trip back he met him. They went to where they had been; the passing of years and the encroaching jungle had obliterated the scars of B-52 strikes and greened over the napalm memories. He also met a young man named Quy who had one leg and no arms and was blinded in one eye. He had triggered a landmine when he was ten. They became friends, but Jack felt he could do little to help.

Such encounters led Jack and Colleen to set up a humanitarian organization, the Fallen Warriors Foundation, which they run out of their basement.

On one of many visits Estes and his foundation members paid to Vietnam, he went with doctors and nurses from Northwest Medical Teams to distribute health supplies, treating 150 patients a day and assessing further needs. On another, in 1998, he accompanied medical personnel to treat the poorest of the poor, sometimes people "who had never seen a doctor, let alone an American one." The Foundation has now provided arms and a leg for Quy; they are sponsoring a young man from Vietnam in Oregon; and they are sending further medical equipment and have plans to build clinics, a well, and toilet facilities for a school. In the United States, they help veterans suffering from post-traumatic stress disorder and hope to establish a video archive of veterans telling their stories of Vietnam. They want to film former enemy soldiers and place the films in libraries across the country as a visual testimony of the tragedy of war. "We believe these films will promote healing and forgiveness and perhaps notify future generations that the tragedy of war doesn't end when the battle is over. It's only just begun."

In 1998 Colleen brought to Oregon a Buddhist monk, Claude Thomas. He is a Vietnam veteran and member of the Zen Peacemaking Order, a student of Thich Nhat Hanh. As a helicopter crew chief, he was shot down five times and wounded. Thomas was originally just intending to conduct a meditation and healing retreat for veterans and their families. But the Fallen Warriors Foundation became involved with the Prison Vietnam Veterans Association and arranged for Thomas to come into a prison and lead a meditation and listening session for a group of men, most of whom were serving sentences for murder. From there they moved to a wildlife sanctuary and held a retreat which, says Jack, was "extraordinarily powerful and healing for all concerned."

"We're not doctors or counselors," Jack says, "but people are constantly looking to us for help." He and Colleen believe a byproduct of helping to heal the scars in Vietnam will be the healing of some of the scars in the United States. "Forgiving our enemies is a step toward healing," says Jack.

A Parable

In recent years audiences have watched a drama of forgiveness played out onstage in the musical version of *Les Miserables*. The musical follows its original source, Victor Hugo's sprawling novel, in telling the story of Jean Valjean, a French prisoner hounded and ultimately transformed by forgiveness.

Sentenced to a nineteen-year term of hard labor for the crime of stealing bread, Jean Valjean gradually hardened into a tough convict. No one could beat him in a fist fight. No one could break his will. At last Valjean earned his release. Convicts in those days had to carry identity cards, however, and no innkeeper would let a dangerous felon spend the night. For days he wandered the village roads, seeking shelter against the weather, until finally a kindly bishop had mercy on him.

That night Jean Valjean lay still in an overcomfortable bed until the bishop and his sister drifted off to sleep. He rose from his bed, rummaged through the cupboard for the fmaily silver, and crept off into the darkness.

The next morning three policemen knocked on the bishop's door, with Valjean in tow. They had caught the convict in flight with the purloined silver, and were ready to put the scoundrel in chains for life.

The bishop responded in a way that no one, especially Valjean, expected.

"So here you are!" he cried to Valjean. "I'm delighted to see you. Had you forgotten that I gave you the candlesticks as well? They're silver like the rest, and worth a good 200 francs. Did you forget to take them?"

Jean Valjean's eyes had widened. He was now staring at the old man with an expression no words can convey.

Valjean was no thief, the bishop assured the gendarmes. "This silver was my gift to him."

When the gendarmes withdrew, the bishop gave the candlesticks to his guest, now speechless and trembling. "Do not forget, do not ever forget," said the bishop, "that you have promised me to use the money to make yourself an honest man."

The power of the bishop's act, defying every human instinct for revenge, changed Jean Valjean's life forever. A naked encounter with forgiveness — especially since he had never repented — melted the granite defenses of his soul. He kept the candlesticks as a precious memento of grace and dedicated himself from then on to helping others in need.

Hugo's novel stands, in fact, as a two-edged parable of forgiveness. A detective named Javert, who knows no law but justice, stalks Jean Valjean mercilessly over the next two decades. As Valjean is transformed by forgiveness, the detective is consumed by thirst for retribution. When Valjean saves Javert's life — the prey showing grace to his pursuer — the detective senses his black-and-white world beginning to crumble. Unable to cope with a grace that goes against all instinct, and finding within himself no corresponding forgiveness, Javert jumps off a bridge into the Seine River.

— Philip Yancey, *What's So Amazing about Grace*

8

Another bridge over the River Kwai: Anglo-Japanese reconciliation

"Forgiveness is the ornament of the brave."

— Sanskrit saying

In May 1998, a news photo went around the world of former British prisoners of war of the Japanese turning their backs on the emperor of Japan and Queen Elizabeth when they rode through London together. This act of discourtesy, testament to persisting bitterness and a legacy of World War II, was probably all that many people heard about the Japanese state visit. According to the *Guardian*, the act "left an indelible image of shock and humiliation on the faces of Japanese VIPs passing them in royal procession."

In that same crowd, however, there were other British veterans of the Southeast Asia campaign — some of whom had been prisoners of war — waving Japanese flags to welcome Emperor Akihito. Their photo did not go out to the world.

Both groups of men may have represented legitimate news stories. But how much it would have meant to the world if the story of continuing bitterness had been accompanied by one of forthright forgiveness!

One answer to the question why some forgive and some do not may lie in the company one keeps. If you move with those who constantly remind you how much you suffered and how bad the other lot were, it is hard to break free. If you associate with those who, despite the sufferings and scars which they share with you, want to move on, it gives you the encouragement to leave the past behind.

One of those in the crowd who waved a Japanese flag, Richard Channer, is part of a British veteran's organization, the Burma Campaign Fellowship Group (BCFG), which was founded specifically to build bridges between former enemies of World War II. It is a fellowship of highly decorated soldiers. The BCFG traces its origins to a Welsh engine driver, Gwilym Davies. He decided in the early 1980s that he wanted to shake the hands of his former enemies. To the horror of his fellow veterans in Aberystwyth — who stopped talking to him and his wife — he made contact with the Japanese embassy in London. They put him in touch with Masao Hirakubo, a Japanese businessman who had fought at the battle of Kohima, where the Japanese forces were halted in Nagaland on the India/Burma border. Hirakubo accompanied Jenkins and another Welsh veteran to Japan, where they met Japanese Burma ex-servicemen and returned even more committed to building bridges, despite further vilification from their comrades. Since then the BCFG has organized exchange visits between British and Japanese veterans and initiated services of reconciliation at Westminster Abbey. And Hirakubo has been decorated by the British and Japanese governments for his work to promote reconciliation between the Japanese Burma Army and British/India 14th Army, comprising Indian, African, and British troops.

Channer, who was wounded at the Battle of Imphal and was awarded the Military Cross, had some years earlier traveled with another British veteran to Kohima to lay wreaths at the British and Indian cemeteries and also beside a tree marking where a Japanese sniper had fought. Their laying a wreath for the thousands of Japanese soldiers who were killed there was described in the *Daily Telegraph* as "one of the more remarkable gestures of reconciliation."

Remembering his experience directing artillery on the gun positions, Channer made himself a megaphone out of cardboard with which he could shout his welcome to the Japanese emperor on the Mall. As the royal party passed, he waved his flag in an arc, and he and two other British ex-servicemen yelled *"Banzai!"* After the procession had passed, one of the protesting servicemen whipped Channer's flag from his hand. Channer's gesture did not go unnoticed. Later that day Independent Television News interviewed him when he waved the Japanese flag outside Westminster Abbey as the Emperor laid a wreath at the Tomb of the Unknown Soldier. Channer had waved the flag that day at the specific request of another BCFG member, Les Dennison.

Les Dennison had been captured at the fall of Singapore in February 1942. The Japanese then took thousands of British and Australian prisoners of war and thousands of Asian laborers to drive a rail link through the mountainous jungle barrier that lay between Thailand and Burma. About twelve thousand POWs and many thousands of the Asian laborers died during its construction. During his three and a half years of incarceration, Dennison watched fourteen of his fellow prisoners decapitated. His weight went down from 160 pounds to 74 pounds.

Dennison, in an article in his local paper, the Coventry *Evening Telegraph* (December 12, 1998), under the headline, "Time to call a truce on long-lasting bitterness," had written:

> Reading the letters and articles demanding compensation and apologies from the Japanese government, I am saddened by the negative display of bitterness and hatred after fifty years.
>
> I write as an 83-year-old ex-serviceman who served in the Far East, was defeated and taken prisoner in Singapore, helped clear up the dead and debris with a handcart in Singapore, had a spell in Changi prison, then back up country to Thailand, then marched 200 miles through swamp and jungle to Soukuria, the death camp. After completing our stint of 15 kilometers of railroad and one of the bridges over the River Kwai, 400 survivors out of 1,600 moved on into Burma.

Yes, I still have nightmares and even imagine the sweet sickly stench of the dead waiting to be burnt on a pyre, rain permitting. But with the passing of 55 years, there has been growth, learning, maturity, caring for wife, family and friends.

In 1962 I reluctantly attended an international conference. Reluctantly, because I learnt there was a Japanese delegation attending. One of the Japanese who spoke before the 800 international delegates, General Sugita, who attended the surrender of Singapore, bowing low said, "I know what happened during the campaign. I can never expect you to forget what happened." Then, bowing once more, he said, "I am sorry. Please forgive me and my nation."

It was then that the healing of bitterness and hatred began. Since then I have experienced the care and friendship of many Japanese who have shown sincere remorse and apologies. ... I find the many unforgettable memories can be lived with in the deep healing peace that is nurtured out of one's basic change of attitude.

In a BBC interview broadcast from Hiroshima on the fiftieth anniversary of the dropping of the atomic bomb, Dennison was asked to describe his wartime experiences. The last question to him: "If you could speak Japanese fluently and were to stand up in front of the Japanese nation on this day, what would you say to them?"

His reply: "I would bow low in humility and I would just beg their forgiveness for my callousness at the time when I heard of the bombs being dropped on the cities of Japan and I would humbly ask their forgiveness for the years of my bitterness, resentment and hatred against the people of Japan. That is what I would simply do."

Before the emperor's visit to Britain, Japanese Prime Minister Ryutaro Hashimoto had apologized in an article in the pages of a London tabloid, the *Sun,* for the atrocities committed against British prisoners in World War II. He expressed "deep remorse and heartfelt apology for the tremendous damage and suffering of that time." The *Sun,* which has had a strong record of hostility to the Japanese over the country's attitude to its war record, accompanied the apology with an editorial in which it stated that it had never published an article as historic as that by the Japanese prime minister. It was not an easy decision but "painful though it might be, we have to try to forget. That task hopefully will be made easier after today's astonishing article by Premier Hashimoto."

The paper reported an overwhelmingly positive response to the prime minister's remarks. Its political editor, Trevor Kavanagh, wrote, "Japanese newspapers and diplomats yesterday hailed the *Sun* for opening a new era in relations with Britain — as our readers backed their PM's call for reconciliation."

The *Sun's* rival, the *Mirror,* ran an article headed, "Honourable race we must not hate." It was written by Tony Parsons, who concluded, "Only the men who personally suffered at the hands of the Japanese — and the families of those men — really have a right to hate them. Anybody else who mouths off about the Japanese is just an armchair warrior. And a closet racist."

In a letter to the *Sun,* the head of the BCFG, John Nunneley, wrote:

> As we war veterans come towards the end of our lives we believe there is one last great service all of us can do for our country; forgive the Japanese for their treatment of our prisoners of war; accept the full apology now made by Prime Minister Hashimoto; and in doing so demonstrate a British nobility of spirit which will allow Britain and Japan to go forward as friends and partners into a new millennium.

Major General Lyall Grant, the BCFG's first chairman, in a letter to the *Times* of London, pointed out that the Japanese received in expiation a terrible punishment, and individuals held responsible for specific crimes were executed. "Japanese crimes were certainly no worse than those of our main opponent and scarcely in the same league as those of one of our major allies. These two nations have both been forgiven and surely it is time that the Japanese, with their many admirable qualities, were made equally welcome. At least that is what a growing number of those who fought against them in Southeast Asia now believe."

A month after the Japanese prime minister's apology, the BCFG published *Tales from the Burma Campaign 1942-1945,* an anthology of sixty stories by its members. The book is dedicated to "reconciliation and lasting friendship between two great nations." It reminds readers that the Burma campaign was the longest and arguably the most ferocious campaign of World War II, with both sides rarely taking prisoners, and with 180,000 Japanese soldiers killed and 70,462 Commonwealth soldiers killed, wounded, taken prisoner, or missing. "That there is a need for reconciliation," writes Nunneley, "is recognized particularly by Britain's older generations who cleave to the Christian ethic of forgiveness and who understand also the benefits which this can bring to the two countries."

In the anthology is a "Message for the Future" from Susumu Nishida, president of the All-Burma Veterans' Association of Japan, who was wounded nine times in the Burma campaign. He writes, "I see it as the inexcusable duty of us war veterans, of all nations which fought in Burma, we who are the survivors of close-action skirmish and daily battle, to explain to new generations the true history and tragedy of war with our prayer that peace may be the reward of those who sacrificed their lives."

In the month before the emperor's visit, a Japanese woman, Keiko Holmes, was decorated for her work of reconciling former British prisoners of war and their captors. The *Times* ran an editorial headed "Forgiveness Frees" about the award by Queen Elizabeth II at Windsor Castle to this Japanese woman, married to an Englishman, who had for some seven years been organizing pilgrimages of former POWs and their families to Japan. It concluded that bitterness is understandable among those who endured hideous atrocities. "But it is damaging — not least when, passed down through the generations, it taints the attitudes of those who were not even alive during the war." Keiko Holmes' investiture, the editorial went on, should be seen as more than simply a diplomatic gesture. "It is a mark of respect for someone who believes that we cannot only learn to forgive, but also to forget."

One member of the BCFG is the author Eric Lomax. His experience indicates that there may be a time and season for forgiveness that sometimes cannot be rushed. In his award-winning book, *The Railway Man,* he describes his experience when he was taken prisoner in Singapore when it fell to the Japanese. As a member of the Royal Corps of Signals, he had helped build an illicit radio, whose discovery brought on two years of dreadful torture, starvation, and distress.

For many years after the war, Lomax allowed his professional life to crowd out his desire to settle old accounts with those who had tortured him at Kanburi. But twenty-five years after the war, when he had retired, the desire to know more about what had happened became more intense than ever. "I had to admit that I wanted to make them pay, pay more than they had already done." The more he thought about it, the more he wanted to do physical damage to the Japanese. "Physical revenge seemed the only adequate recompense for the anger I carried." The faces of the Japanese military police were with him every day. But the inter-preter who had been present at all the torture sessions became his "private obsession" and the focus of his hatred.

"Although I could not have admitted it," he says, "I was still fighting the war in all those years of peace."

Then, in an extraordinary sequence of events, Lomax received news of that interpreter, Nagase Takashi, who had appar-ently devoted his life to charitable causes near Kanburi and had just built a Buddhist temple there. Lomax read about his activities, including the organizing of a meeting of reconciliation at the River Kwai bridge, with what he calls "cold skepticism" and found the very thought of Nagase distasteful. "I had not seen a Japanese since 1945 and had no wish ever to meet one again. His reconciliation assembly sounded to me like a fraudulent publicity stunt."

Lomax then encountered a new organization, the Medical Foundation for the Care of Victims of Torture. Like most former POWs, he had not contemplated meeting with psychiatrists or psychotherapists. The Medical Foundation was started by Helen

Bamber, a nurse who entered Bergen-Belsen with the Allies at the age of nineteen in 1945.

In 1989 Lomax was shown an article about the interpreter Nagase, who had devoted much of his life "to making up for the Japanese Army's treatment of prisoners of war." He was quoted as saying that he had decided to dedicate the rest of his life to the memory of those who died constructing the railroad. The article described his ill health, and how every time he had a cardiac arrest he had flashbacks of the Japanese military police torturing a POW who was accused of possessing a map of the railway. "As a former member of the Japanese Army, I thought the agony was what I have to pay for our treatment of POWs."

The POW described was Lomax. At last, Lomax had found one of his tormentors. The old feelings of revenge rose up, and he wanted to damage Nagase for his part in ruining his life. One or two people suggested that it was time to forgive and forget. "I don't normally argue openly about anything, but I began to argue just a little about this. The majority of people who hand out advice about forgiveness have not gone through that sort of experience I had; I was not inclined to forgive, not yet, and probably never."

Then Lomax read an account written by Nagase in which he expressed the belief that he was forgiven. Lomax's wife, Patti, with his agreement, wrote to Nagase expressing astonishment that he could feel forgiven when this man he had tortured had not forgiven him. It was the beginning of a moving exchange of letters which led eventually to their meeting in Kanburi.

Lomax describes the first encounter in these words:

> He began a formal bow, his face working and agitated, the small figure barely reaching my shoulder. I stepped forward and took his hand and said, *"Ohayo gozaimasu, Nagase san, ogenki des ka?"* "Good morning, Mr. Nagase, how are you?"
>
> He looked up at me; he was trembling, in tears, saying over and over "I am very, very sorry ..." I somehow took command, led him out of the terrible heat to a bench in the shade; I was comforting him, for he was really overcome.

At that moment my capacity for reserve and self-control helped me to help him, murmuring reassurances as we sat down. It was as though I was protecting him from the force of the emotions shaking his frail-seeming body. I think I said something like "That's very kind of you to say so" to his repeated expressions of sorrow.

He said to me "Fifty years is a long time, but for me it is a time of suffering. I never forgot you, I remember your face, especially your eyes." He looked deep into my eyes when he said this. His own face still looked like the one I remembered, rather fine-featured, with dark and slightly hidden eyes; his wide mouth was still noticeable beneath cheeks that had sunken inwards.

I told him that I could remember his very last words to me. He asked what they were and laughed when I said "Keep your chin up."

He asked if he could touch my hand. My former interrogator held my hand, which was so much larger than his, stroking it quite unselfconsciously. I didn't find it embarrassing. He gripped my wrist with both of his hands and told me that when I was being tortured — he used the word — he measured my pulse. I remembered he had written this in his memoir. Yet now that we were face to face, his grief seemed far more acute than mine. "I was a member of Imperial Japanese Army; we treated your countrymen very, very badly." "We both survived," I said encouragingly, really believing it now.

A little later, I'm sure he said, "For what purpose were you born in this world? I think I can die safely now."

The two men had long conversations as they moved around the area. Lomax began to feel that his strange companion was a person who he would have been able to get on with long ago if they had met under other circumstances. They had much in common. But Lomax still had the matter of forgiveness to consider. A Thai woman had explained to him the importance of forgiveness in Buddhism:

I understood that whatever you do you get back in life and if what you have done is tainted with evil and you have not made atonement for it, evil is returned to you in the next life with interest. Nagase dreaded hell, and it seemed that our first meeting had made parts of both our lives hellish already. Even if I could not grasp the theology fully, I could no longer see the point of punishing Nagase by a refusal to reach out and forgive him … the question was now one of choosing the right moment to say the words to him with the formality that the situation seemed to demand.

The two men flew to Japan. They went to Hiroshima, and Lomax and Patti laid a bunch of mixed flowers on the memorial. In a Tokyo room, Lomax gave the formal forgiveness Nagase sought. "I told him that while I could not forget what happened in Kanburi in 1943, I assured him of my total forgiveness."

Lomax says that meeting turned Nagase from a hated enemy, with whom friendship would have been unthinkable, into a blood-brother. "In all the time I spent in Japan I never felt a flash of the anger I had harbored against Nagase all those years, no backwash of that surge of murderous intent I had felt on finding that one of them was still alive." The last words of *The Railway Man,* "Sometime the hating has to stop."

Forgiveness, as an act of love, is felt, not achieved. It can be given, but it may not always be received. It cannot be bestowed as either a triumph over another person, or as the means to secure their humiliation or acquiescence.

It is most healing, most profound when it grows out of humility and realism, a hard-won sense that, whether you are entirely to blame in these events and I am blameless, there is in each of us insufficiencies and imperfections that can be our greatest teachers.

You may not recognize forgiveness even when you have experienced it, for what we are seeking to know better is subtle, difficult to define, multi-layered and contains an element of magic. You will, however, feel it in your body. Something — very nearly a "thing" — has left you. You are no longer carrying the load you were; you have put it down. Anger may have given way to sorrow and regret. Rage may have flattened out into indifference or pity. Into what seemed black and white has crept a little grey.

The muscular tensions that you had come to assume were normal are eased. You are less vulnerable to infection or to far more serious illness. Your immune system lifts. Your face muscles let down. Food tastes better. The world looks better. You are more available to other people and a great deal more available to yourself, yet you think about yourself less, and less anxiously.

Stephanie Dowrick
Forgiveness and Other Acts of Love

Another well-known writer who suffered horrific wartime experiences in a Japanese prison camp was Laurens van der Post. Few foreigners have better succeeded in living into the minds and hearts of the Japanese. Few have been more sensitive to a dimension of life that transcends the usual humdrum existence of most people and creates a bond between people of all backgrounds. He lived for a time in Japan and knew how much the degrees and nuances of polite speech mattered to the Japanese.

In his autobiographical odyssey, *Yet Being Someone Other,* van der Post describes an occasion in Java when, completely unarmed, he was surprised by Japanese troops who charged him with fixed bayonets. Something in him took over command, he says, and enabled him to call out in Japanese, and in a Japanese degree of politeness he wasn't even conscious of remembering, that transfixed his attackers, and saved his life and those of others. "From that moment on," he writes, "that other voice was increasingly all that stood between me and death. At every stage the crisis of instant death and a final sentence of execution was repeated, and it was resolved only by this other person in me."

He credits the effect of this "other voice" with planting the seeds of an integrity which imposed on vast, disordered prisons of alienated and embittered men of all nations and services a self-imposed order and creativity which allowed many of them to survive their ordeal. He also underlines his realization of the link between his instinctive impulse to invite two Japanese to have coffee at a table with him, and the way he later saved his own life and those of thousands of others in the war. This event had shown him that no life, however humble — no detail, however insignificant — was without universal importance.

It is van der Post's contention that he and his fellow prisoners had come out of prison profoundly different from what they had been before, "and totally bereft of bitterness and of longing either for revenge or for an exercise of uncomprehending fundamentalist justice."

At the time of the funeral of Emperor Akihito's father, Emperor Hirohito, when there had also been controversy, this time over the rightness of Britain being represented, van der Post wrote to the *Times* that he did not wish to sit in judgment on those who felt they could not forgive and would carry their sense of injury to the grave with a dignity of total silence. But he also did not feel that even those who could not forgive would want to feed the "diatribe and strange hysteria" that existed among people who had not been in prison, and some who were not born at the time. He wrote, "Wing Commander Nichols and I, with a remarkable nucleus of officers and men of all three services, brought some 2,000 men out of prison. Nichols said he could count on the fingers of two hands those who were bitter and unforgiving."

Van der Post said he marveled at how men who never endured war at all could exploit the suffering of more than forty years ago and pursue it almost as a means of entertainment. "The men for whom I speak, and the majority of our friends who have died since our release, found a meaning in their suffering which reduced the pain of its impact to nothing and sent them back not to form gangs of the spirit, and institutions with a vested interest in the suffering which was their justification, but as individuals who have now made a far greater contribution to the life of our time than they would have done without the dark privilege conferred on them through suffering."

9

From Grini to the Gulag: Strengthened by prison experiences

"I thought that the only hope for the world lay in an all-embracing attitude of forgiveness of the people who had been our enemies. Forgiveness, my prison experience had taught me, was not mere religious sentimentality; it was as fundamental a law of the human spirit as the law of gravity. If one broke the law of gravity one broke one's neck; if one broke this law of forgiveness one inflicted a mortal wound on one's spirit and became once again a member of the chain gang of mere cause and effect from which life has labored so long and so painfully to escape."

— Laurens van der Post, *The Night of the New Moon*

The experience of prison can embitter and envenom a person as easily as it can ennoble them, David Aikman points out, writing about Nelson Mandela: "Yet how imprisonment shaped a zealous revolutionary into a great statesman over twenty-seven years, endowing him with a moral stature that was recognized even by his political adversaries, is one of the great stories of grace in the twentieth century." He was a different person. He had not deviated an iota from his ultimate goal of a multiracial regime in which black voters had rights identical to those of whites. "But he sought it now in a very different spirit. Above all else, he radiated forgiveness." Mandela says, "I came out mature."

In varying degrees that has been the experience of men and women in many countries. Russian Irina Ratushinskaya was imprisoned because of her poetry when she was only twenty-eight years old. She nearly died from malnutrition and the hunger strikes she endured to call attention to the abuse of human rights. She had received the longest sentence for political crime for any woman in the Soviet Union since the days of Stalin — seven years of hard labor to be followed by five years of internal exile. Her work was regarded as particularly dangerous because people would learn and recite her poems. After four years she was released under pressure from the West, just before the Reykjavik summit.

Ratushinskaya says that she and other former prisoners of totalitarian regimes are endlessly asked why they do not sound bitter about the past. And when they try to explain that in a way it was a positive experience, people make strange faces and ask what is so positive about suffering.

There is a bond of understanding among those who have been in prison, particularly those who have been in solitary confinement, and in many cases there is a forgiving spirit. And experiences and insights that others want to hear. South African bishop Stanley Mogoba, for instance, said, "On Robben Island it was difficult to forgive the people who were doing so much to you. However feelings of anger eat you up more than the other person."

Corrie ten Boom, who was imprisoned in Ravensbrück, described seeing one of her guards in a congregation in Munich after the war. He came up to her after she spoke and put out his hand, saying that Jesus had washed away his sins. Corrie, who had preached forgiveness, wondered how she could give it to someone who had behaved so badly, but she discovered that when God tells us to love our enemies, he gives the love itself along with the command. She said, "You never so touch the ocean of God's love as when you forgive and love your enemies."

The first lesson one immediately learns after being arrested, says Ratushinskaya, is about hatred. She and her fellow prisoners were given cause to hate every day, enticed by entirely unwarranted slights and hurts. Until she was in prison, she could not understand why Jesus spoke out so strongly against hatred. But those in prison who were not able to throw away their hatred sometimes became insane. In ordinary life, she explains, if you are angry you can think about something else. But the KGB did not allow such an easy escape. The most practical escape the prisoners found was to find something funny in the situation, to feel sorry for the guards, to corrupt them without saying a word except "good morning."

The day Ratushinskaya came home from prison, she offered her KGB escort a cup of coffee. "If you start to hate," she says, "you can never stop. You can burn yourself from inside. To retain one's personality, to survive, simply to keep common sense, one has to kill hatred, immediately."

There is a group of people who, in terms of human justification, could have every reason to hate — those who were taken hostage in the Middle East. For eight years, from 1984 to 1991, more than a dozen men suffered in cells, sometimes alone, sometimes with others, not knowing what was to become of them. Terry Waite, the archbishop of Canterbury's envoy, says that he has slowly begun to understand Christ's wisdom. "'Love your neighbor' is hard when it lands on your own shoulders. The growing up to faith through the darkness happens slowly, in God's time. And a deeper touch with God and with others grows. Even my mother-in-law now says, 'You're a bit more human.' I am sure now that it takes no courage to put a bullet into your enemy. It takes much courage to believe that light and life are stronger than darkness."

Jerry Levin, who was CNN's Beirut bureau chief, was chained for long excruciating months to a radiator and kept blindfolded in solitary confinement. He told his wife, "I forgave them as I began to see how bitter and desperate they were." He says, "Here I was an obvious pawn in the hands of angry extremists. I had to forgive them because my captivity had forced me to take this spiritual journey. And in forgiving my captors I could proceed, free of the baggage of hate, resentment, fear and revenge. If that was God's reason for putting me in solitary confinement, I thank him. And I thank him for my Jewish parents, my Christian wife and family and my Muslim friends. The prayers from all three faiths sustained me." His wife, Sis, author of *Beirut Diary,* admits the turmoil she sometimes feels when taking communion, knowing she must be freed from any shadow of resentment. "Forgiveness is not some sticky sentimental thing. It's very pragmatic. I never said it was easy, but nothing else works."

Brian Keenan, from Northern Ireland, who had been a lecturer in Beirut, spoke along with other ex-hostages at an occasion in Derry, attended by representatives of the different divisions of Ireland, including President Mary Robinson. Its theme was "Beyond hate — living with our deepest differences." He told his audience that what was needed was to go beyond self-preoccupation to finding a revolutionary love. "I cannot condemn a man because he is different from me. By the degree he is different I am enlarged and expanded. I know that I make history in every touch I have with people, even how I greet people in the street."

In his autobiography *An Evil Cradling,* Keenan describes how he was moved seventeen times in four and a half years and spent three years chained at ankle and wrist. He writes of a captor: "I could see the man not defined by Islam or by ethnic background, perhaps a man more confined than the man in chains; a man more hurt and anguished than the man he had just beaten. These men existed in their own kind of prison, perhaps more confining than the one that held us." He adds, "Each of us had to reach inside himself to find that which was necessary to survive."

Terry Anderson, who was AP bureau chief in the Middle East and spent 2,454 days in captivity, says that for a while he hated, but then he began to get to know his captors as they talked of their families and countries. "Slowly they became people to me." When you had nothing but a blank wall to look at, you started to probe yourself, to look inside your own motives, your own actions. And that is where the healing began, where you began to understand and to move beyond hate. "I know this now, that if I am in confrontation with another person, another group, I cannot first ask anything of the other side, even if I feel that I am the victim. It doesn't have to be the oppressor who has to take the first step; it is the oppressed who can say: 'I forgive.'"

Out of prison

Satan is a name we use
For darkness in the world,
A goat on which we load
Our most horrific sins
To carry off our guilt.
But all the evil I have seen
was done by human beings.
It isn't a dark angel
Who rigs a car into a bomb,
Or steals money meant for other's food.
And it wasn't any alien spirit
That chained me to this wall.

One of those who kidnapped me
Said once: "No man believes he's evil."
A penetrating and subtle thought
In these circumstances, and from him.
And that's the mystery:
He's not stupid, and doesn't seem insane.
He knows I've done no harm to him or his.
He's looked into my face
Each day for years, and
Heard me crying in the night.
Still he daily checks my chain,
Makes sure my blindfold is secure,
Then kneels outside my cell
And prays to Allah, merciful, compassionate.

I know too well the darker urges in myself,
The violence and the selfishness.
I've seen little in him I can't recognize.
I also know my mind would shatter,
My soul would die if I did the things he does.
I'm tempted to believe there really is
A devil in him, some malefic,
Independent force that makes him
Less or other than a man.
That's too easy and too dangerous an answer;
It's how so many evils come to be.
I must reject, abhor and fight against
These acts, and acknowledge that
They're not unhuman — just the opposite.
We can't separate the things
We do from what we are;
Hate the sin and love the sinner is not
A concept I'll ever really understand.

I'll never love him — I'm not Christ.
But I'll try to achieve forgiveness
Because I know that in the end,
As always, Christ was right.

— Terry Anderson

Father Lawrence Jenco, from the Servite Order, was working in a relief agency in Lebanon when he was taken hostage. As he stepped from a car in Rome within days of his release from captivity, a photographer shouted at him from a distance, "Father Jenco, what are you feeling towards the terrorists who held you?"

He responded without much thought: "I'm a Christian. I must forgive them." The sentiment had been in his heart for some time.

"I had come to understand that my captors could not be my enemies. They had to be my brothers. Through his life and through his final agony, Jesus taught us that the heart of love is forgiveness. This is what he asked of us. This is what he asked of me during my captivity." In some ways, Father Jenco found it harder to forgive what he felt was inadequate responses to his plight by the U.S. government and his church than he did the cruelty of his captors. "Having forgiven," he says, "I am liberated. I need no longer be determined by the past."

Toward the end of Jenco's captivity, one of his guards, a man named Sayeed who had at times brutalized him, sat down on the mat with him. He had recently started calling him "Abouna," an Arabic name meaning "dear father." At first he was "Jenco," then "Lawrence," then "Abouna," indicating by the change of voice that a change of heart was taking place. Sayeed asked if Jenco remembered the first six months of his captivity. Jenco responded, "Yes, Sayeed. I remember all the pain and suffering you caused me and my brothers." Then Sayeed asked, "Abouna, do you forgive me?"

In his book *Bound To Forgive,* Jenco records his response:

> These quietly spoken words overwhelmed me. As I sat blindfolded, unable to see the man who had been my enemy, I understood I was called to forgive, to let go of revenge, retaliation, and forgive.
>
> And I was challenged to forgive him unconditionally. I could not forgive him on the condition that he change his behavior to conform to my wishes or values. I had no control over his response. I understood I was to say yes.
>
> I said, "Sayeed, there were times I hated you. I was filled with anger and revenge for what you did to me and my brothers. But Jesus said on a mountain top that I was not to hate you. I was to love you. Sayeed, I need to ask God's forgiveness and yours."

Father Jenco reflected on numerous scriptural passages: "Forgive and you will be forgiven" (Luke); "Whenever you stand praying, forgive, if you have anything against anyone" (John); and, in the Sermon on the Mount, the reminder by Jesus that if while presenting their offerings before an altar they remembered their brother or sister had something against them, they should first go and be reconciled with their brother and sister. Also in the Hebrew covenant, the sage author, the son of Sirach, wrote, "Forgive your neighbor the wrong he has done, and then your sins will be pardoned when you pray."

Father Jenco wrote these and other passages in his journal:

> Writing them down was the easy part, making them incarnate was no easy task. The scene between Sayeed and me depicted two prodigal sons coming together. Sayeed asked for my forgiveness. I asked God and Sayeed to forgive me my anger and hate, my desire to punish and get revenge. This was a graced moment. Two men, alienated brothers, off in our own alien lands, eating the silage of bitterness and resentment, embraced. Two sons came home to their hearts, in which the spirit of peace and reconciliation lives. It was a transforming moment of mutual forgiveness and healing of hurts. The gift of the moment moved us from alienation to reconciliation, and from brokenness to wholeness before God.

When Father Jenco offered Sayeed his forgiveness, he knew intuitively he had been set free and could go home. He had empowered himself with God's word, "Be kind and tenderhearted to one another and forgive one another as I the God of both of you have forgiven you." "In the quietness of the night I would hear the counsel of my brother Servite, Neal Flanagan. I remember him telling me, 'If you want to see what hate does, you should go to Northern Ireland. Hate even changes your physical appearance.'"

A few days before his release, another young guard who had earlier threatened him with death put his hands on the priest's shoulders and massaged them. "I wished I could have looked into his eyes, which on that first day had been eyes of hate, for I felt that this had become the touch of love."

In a letter prepared for his possible execution, Father Jenco wrote, "Dear brothers and sisters, if I am to die, I hope that I would die with the words of Jesus on my lips: 'Father, forgive them; for they do not know what they are doing.' Please do not hate them." He was, fortunately, spared.

The two men who follow in this chapter have to an extraordinary degree come out of the prison ordeal, and the experience of forgiveness both strengthened and with a sense of mission.

As ambassador to the United States, and a representative of Somalia at the United Nations and other international bodies, Dr. Yusuf Omar al-Azhari led what he calls "a golden life." A son-in-law of his country's president, he thought that no one could ever change it, but one day "the hour of accountability" caught up with him.

His father-in-law was assassinated and a military junta took over the country, a junta dedicated to scientific socialism. Summoned home from Washington, al-Azhari was soon arrested and imprisoned for four and a half months. He was transferred to a military camp to be trained in Marxism and then sent to work as a farm laborer. Passing all the tests, as he puts it, he was made director-general at the Ministry of Information and National Guidance. Though suspect in the eyes of the regime, he kept his post for nearly two years and then was appointed ambassador to Nigeria. At a reception for a visiting Soviet delegation, he was heard making critical remarks and was summoned back to Mogadishu.

A year later al-Azhari was picked up at home at three o'clock in the morning, handcuffed, blindfolded, taken 350 kilometers into the countryside, and put in a cell three meters by four meters in area. He was to remain in that cell, in solitary confinement, with "nothing to read, no one to talk to, and no one to listen to," for six years. For the first six months of his imprisonment he was tortured daily and, as he says, possessed by torment, anger, hate, depression and violence. His health deteriorated; he became skin and bones and was afraid that he would have a stroke or become insane or die. "My brain was trying to burst."

Then one night, al-Azhari recalls, he knelt down at eight in the evening, soaked with tears, and asked for guidance from the Almighty Creator to give him peace within himself and a purpose to guide him. When he finally got up from his knees, it was four o'clock in the morning. "Eight hours had passed as if it were eight minutes. I was exalted spiritually in my cell. I never had a better eight hours of prayer in my life," he says.

The inner voice told him, "Be honest to yourself and those around you and you will be the happiest person on earth. Don't limit yourself to earthly matters only, go beyond that." From that day on, fear had no place in his life. "I was cured and freed of hate, anger, despair, depression and the desire for earthly greed and enjoyment only. It was as if I had found a new identity. From then on I was accountable with honesty for all my actions."

The next day the guards found a new person, calm, brotherly, submissive. They could not torture him as before. "How could I have changed overnight? they asked me." He decided to accept prison life instead of fighting against it, dividing the hours into time for physical exercise and time to conduct debates with himself about his past. He would spend hours thinking back over the wrongs he had done in his life, devoting a day to each item that occurred to him, but also tracing back the good things "so that I was not obsessed." Knowing the horrible things, he says, "I would never turn to that but be reconciled to poor and rich, to those who need help." Six years in prison gave him a training in life he could not have received in any other way. "When I look at the scars I carry, they don't remind me of the evil things done to me but I see beyond them."

In January 1991 the Supreme Revolutionary Council which had taken over the country was finally deposed. The commander-in-chief of the armed forces, Major General Mohammed Siad Barré, fled to Nigeria, where he was given sanctuary. Emerging from prison, al-Azhari went to search for his family. He found them living in a hut in Mogadishu. "When my wife saw me with a long beard standing at the door, she fainted. She had been told that I had been shot and killed trying to escape. She had no idea I had been imprisoned."

"Can you forgive a man who has done that?" Ambassador al-Azhari asked at a 1996 conference in South Africa with the theme, "Healing the past, building the future." "Can you forgive a man who has killed your father-in-law and put you in a cell where you could become a vegetable or mad or even dead and who has never asked for forgiveness? That's a big challenge."

One day, while sitting in a coffee shop, he was overwhelmed by a feeling that he should forgive this man who had caused him so much misery. It took him two years to decide to do so. "I asked for guidance and found I could no longer resist the need to forgive." But how to get a ticket to Nigeria? Al-Azhari had no money: his bank account had been confiscated, and his land auctioned off. Three days later he was asked unexpectedly to represent his country at a UN conference in West Africa and was able to visit the eighty-seven-year-old former dictator. "I went all the way there just to tell him, while he was still alive, that I forgave him. I cannot express how emotional he became at that moment. I could see tears flowing down his cheeks. I thanked God for letting me fill the heart of such a man with remorse. He said to me, 'Thank you. You have cured me. I can sleep tonight knowing that people like you exist in Somalia.'"

Ambassador al-Azhari is working, without any official position, to bring peace and reconciliation to his country — a country without a government, a judicial system, police, or schools, where at least 40 percent of the children between one and ten years of age have died or been killed. He persists despite being shot at and wounded, and he is sustained by his prison experience. "Love had been planted in my heart and I vowed there to serve my fellow countrymen and women, poor and rich, to reconcile and settle their differences with harmony, love and forgiveness." He says that the forgiveness factor created in him humility and self-confidence and the realization that he could befriend anyone without any complex. "It prepared me and taught me how to approach a person or a group of people whether they are foes or friends. It became a way of life to me. It is an instrument that one can use to defuse tension, grievances or misunderstandings. It is an honest method to win the hearts of others."

Al-Azhari says that because of the deep-rooted mistrust and animosity created by the civil war, "the forgiveness factor is the only criterion that could bring adversaries together." In 1994, with the help of Swedish facilitation, he and sixteen other Somalis representing warlords from different warring factions met alone in a villa at Stensnäs outside Stockholm. It was soon clear to them that unless they were going to go on killing each other, they had to find a way out of the political impasses, that they had to honestly address the issues.

Al-Azhari, with the experience of his forgiveness of Siad Barré behind him, felt he should make the first move. He decided to forgive those present whom he had hated and asked their forgiveness. Friendship and trust began to grow.

They then moved to Uppsala where they were joined by northern Somali brothers who had not been present at Stensnäs. On behalf of the southerners, al-Azhari asked forgiveness of the northerners over matters about which they were aggrieved. "Our conference was turned from one of confrontation and dialogue only to one of repentance," he says. "From that day on the forgiveness factor has been playing a major role in the reconciliation process in Somalia."

Attempts to collectively solve the Somali political deadlock failed, he has said, but through the guidance of Allah, the "peacemakers," whose numbers are now substantial, conceived a new approach:

> We came to the conclusion that to solve the problem from top down was at present impossible due to the complexity of what had happened during the civil war; of the bloodshed, deep-rooted clan hatred, mistrust and antagonism.

> We assumed that it would be much easier to start the healing from the bottom up, from the village level. Introducing the forgiveness factor, we were able to create an atmosphere of confidence and trust among the village clans. Our task to reach the heart of everyone, with the grace of Allah, became easier.

It was decided to create an administrative unit of Puntland out of the northeastern regions, with a view to one day establishing a federal republic of Somalia. Al-Azhari says that he and Abdullahi Yusuf, the chairman and founder of the SSDF (Somali Salvation Democratic Front), had, with the help of the guidance of Allah, come to the conclusion that they should not seek office in the new administration and government. "We also agreed that we would seek forgiveness from everyone that was hurt in any way by us. He forgave all those to whom he had any sort of ill-feeling."

Al-Azhari says that the response they got from the elected representatives from the five regions of Puntland was like a miracle. "Everybody seemed stunned at the beginning, not expecting such humility from the SSDF chairman. In fact, Abdullahi was nominated and reelected with a large margin to head the Puntland administration. God acts in a strange and positive way when one listens and obeys."

In establishing Puntland, they did not think that everything would successfully fall into place. They knew that there would be difficulties and confrontations. "But the will of Allah was there. Human planning and intentions had little to do with the magnitude of what has been accomplished. It was a 'godlike' happening that grew step by step out of the guidance of Almighty the Creator."

"You cannot imagine how spiritually exulted I feel," he says, "whenever I bring together antagonistic groups to forgive each other and live peacefully together in Somalia. I see no other factor that could be implemented constructively in Somalia than forgiveness to heal the past for a long time to come."

In 1943 Leif Hovelsen was a prisoner in solitary confinement in a condemned cell in the infamous Gestapo prison in Oslo, and later in the Grini concentration camp. A teenager in the Norwegian Resistance, he had been betrayed, captured, tortured and condemned to death.

More than fifty years later, the only evidence of those horrific experiences is deafness from Gestapo beatings. Hovelsen has led a fulfilled life which has vitally affected thousands of people, particularly in Germany and Russia. He puts it down to forgiveness. "It all goes back to my experience in prison and in the camp. God gave me life. It was for a purpose. I'm not bogged down with bitterness or bad feelings about people. It's a wonderful gift."

Saved from execution by the ending of the war, Hovelsen found himself shortly after the liberation with roles reversed as one of the guards taking it out on his former captors, including the camp commandant. He did so with enthusiasm, humiliating them with the same punishment drills they had inflicted on him. A security officer, Wilhelm Heilman, begged Hovelsen for some water as he was sweating and thirsty. Hovelsen took a bucketful and threw it in his face. His Norwegian comrades laughed. But he had an uncomfortable feeling as he went home that he had done something wrong. His conscience told him, "There is no excuse. What you did was rotten."

"I knew inside it was true and I despised myself," he says. "I wanted to fight for right and justice, but this was lust for revenge. It hurts to see the naked truth about oneself. In my own nature, as a Christian and a Norwegian patriot, I had the same evil demons in me for which I was accusing National Socialism and the Germans."

As he was walking in the hills one day, the young Norwegian got to thinking about the Gestapo agent who had tortured him, and suddenly, clearly and unexpectedly there came the thought, "Tell him you forgive him." It had never crossed Hovelsen's mind before; it was totally outside his world; but it was, he says, an inner imperative. "If people hear about it," he thought at the time, "they will think I'm a nut." His mother encouraged the idea. "Say that I am praying for him," she said.

So when it next came Hovelsen's turn to do guard duty, he summoned the man and they stood face to face. "He knew me," remembers the Norwegian, "and his glance was uneasy. I looked him in the eye and said words that had come to me and added what my mother had said. He shook all over but did not say anything, and I put him back in his cell."

Later, on the strength of evidence provided by others, the man was condemned to death and executed. But Hovelsen is pleased that before he died the German Gestapo officer asked to take Communion. "If God opened himself to this man, that means that before God, he and I are equal. And I have no right to condemn or accuse someone else."

Through that step of forgiving, Hovelsen was freed from the past and actually went to Germany soon after the end of the war, stretching out the hand of friendship to his former enemies. His work helped pave the way for the first visit to Norway after the war of a West German cabinet minister and of the West German head of state.

In later years Hovelsen befriended Soviet dissidents, helping Andrei Sakharov get the Nobel Peace Prize. He wrote to one dissident:

> Anyone can be given the gift of being a free man, free of hate, revenge and bitterness. What happened to me was a divine intervention. At the moment when I acted on the compelling thought that had come to me, I neither understood nor grasped what I did, nor did I fully realize how deep my fear and hate against the Gestapo and the Germans were. But by obeying, I became a free person. And because of that I was used in an amazing way to build reconciliation between our two countries.

In the 1990s Hovelsen made many trips to Russia, helping to shore up the moral and spiritual infrastructure of that country. He was interviewed on national television about this experience of forgiving the Germans after the war. One interviewer told him that forgiving your enemies was the most important question in Russia. He told an interviewer for *Literaturnaya Gazeta* that what he had done in 1945 was illogical and unpopular but providential. "It was the salvation for the Gestapo man who was executed because of his crimes but who found peace with his maker and victory over death. It has also become a door-opening experience to so many people — Germans, Poles, Russians — in their struggle to find inner freedom and deliverance from the evil of hate."

Over the years Hovelsen has developed a wide perspective. "We in our generation, and those older, have never faced that we were also responsible for the Holocaust in the sense that we didn't have the moral and spiritual insight to see it coming and the political will to do something to stop it. Instead we in our countries adopted the spirit of Munich."

He sums up what has happened to him: "When I answered the Nazis with the same treatment meted out to me, their spirit had conquered me. When I forgave I had conquered National Socialism."

In 1997, fifty-two years after the war, there was a sequel to this story. For the first time, Hovelsen wondered what had happened to the camp guard Heilman. "God's spirit touches you in the middle of the night," he says. "Suddenly you see another side you had overlooked or were not ready to see." Indeed, the Norwegian had never reflected on the effect his action had had on the German. Deep down he had considered what the German had done was worse than what he himself had done. He hadn't included himself as part of the wrong. "So many accuse others for the evil they do," he says, "but refuse to see that we ourselves might be part of it. Whatever I did of evil I am responsible for a need to restore if possible."

He decided to go to Germany to seek out Heilman. After a huge search, eliminating dozens of other Wilhelm Heilmans, he got on the trail and eventually discovered that his captor had died five years earlier. He learned that while Heilman was in the Norwegian occupation, his father, mother, and four sisters had been killed in a British bombing raid on Germany.

Finally, he located Heilman's surviving daughter. "I met your father in Norway," he told her in their first phone conversation. "I have been looking for him because I so much wanted to talk to him."

"What did you want to talk about?" she asked.

"We were not friends. He was a guard and I was a prisoner," he replied. Then he told her the story about the punishment drill and the bucketful of water, and that he had realized how wrong he had been. "I wanted to tell your father how sorry I have been and to ask for his forgiveness."

There was a moment's silence, and then she said with a firm, clear voice, "I forgive you and I know my father would have too."

A few weeks later, Hovelsen went together with the daughter and her husband to Heilman's grave. He placed three roses there. He says, "Standing there, I knew God had healed the wounds of the past, the evil that I had inflicted on an enemy and on myself."

Hovelsen says that many of his generation were raised on Darwin, Marx, Freud, and a faith in limitless progress. "We were so spellbound by our rigid world view that we did not make any room for the moral and spiritual powers that exist beyond us; nor did we accept evil as a reality in or around us." That shortsightedness, he believes, led to much evil and destruction, and it is his hope that today's generation will find a deeper understanding of human nature and the continuous battle between good and evil which is raging in the world. "Only a commitment to choosing what is right," he says, "can make the twenty-first century a redeemed one."

Hovelsen sees forgiveness as a gift, a fruit of obedience to the truth God reveals in your heart:

I didn't realize I had hate in my heart. By obeying he took out that seed of hate and put in a seed of love. He did something for me I didn't recognize until later. When I came to Germany I was a free man. That freedom opened the hearts of Germans to what I could share with them. They sensed something in me and my affection for them. That opened the hearts of Germans for deep talks, and I had many, many deep talks.

My life experience is that when you honestly try to do the mending, God does the healing. I cannot explain why I was saved from execution. My response has been to try to follow the inner voice as a priority. Many strange things happen. Life has not been my kind of choice. It was God who made it. One way I have chosen. On the other hand it has been chosen for me. If I've had any strength, it is that I have chosen to be chosen.

10

Peace dividends: Spokespersons for a new way of thinking

"Forgiveness is not just an occasional act: it is a permanent attitude."

— Martin Luther King, Jr.

Eliezer Cifuentes, from Guatemala, is lucky to be alive. One night in 1980, four carloads of military police ambushed his car and shot him. With a bullet in his arm and crouching low in his car, using the outlines of houses to steer by, he managed to evade his pursuers, then jettisoned his car, ran, and found shelter in a shop for five hours. At midnight, borrowing the shopkeeper's car and disguised as a woman, he drove back to Guatemala City and found asylum in the Costa Rican embassy. After four months of negotiations, he was allowed to fly to San José.

In exile, his hatred of his would-be killers grew. He could not bear to see a policeman; he had terrible headaches. Then one day he had an experience that transformed his life when he recognized "the tigers of hatred" in his heart for the military and for the United States, which he felt was backing them. He realized that he had not practiced the love that he had often preached. "I found a renewal inside that began to change my feelings of hatred and my desire for vengeance."

Cifuentes says, "Giving up hatred is a wonderful, personal experience, but my danger was to leave it at that." He decided to go and see a former Guatemalan intelligence officer, who he thought was responsible for drawing up the lists of intended kidnap victims. Eventually, as they had further meetings, he was able to be honest about his hatred of the military. This led to changes of attitude on both sides and to a meeting outside the country with senior army officers, who expressed their readiness to work with him for national reconciliation. After a struggle, his wife, Clemencia, and their children also decided to forgive.

Renée Pan is a Buddhist nun whose husband, the deputy prime minister of Cambodia, was murdered by the Khmer Rouge when they took over the country in 1975. She escaped to the United States, where she struggled to become economically independent. But over time she felt that her mind had been consumed by what her Buddhist religion calls the "three fires of the world" — greed, anger, and foolishness.

At a low point, when she felt her heart was numb and her brain empty, she had an experience that led her to treat the Khmer Rouge differently. She says, "It was very hard for me to forgive the Khmer Rouge for what they did to me, my family and my friends, and especially to my beloved country. But the burden of revenge that I carried for a decade was lightened from the moment that I did so."

Abeba Tesfagiorgis, an author from Eritrea, was suspected by the Ethiopian occupiers of her country of being in the underground resistance. She was imprisoned and at one point even faced a firing squad. In prison she came face to face with the man who had betrayed her. She forgave him. She tried to help the other prisoners see that it would be a disservice to their fallen comrades if they did not forgive their enemies. "We all pray together for our release and peace," she told them, "but God will not answer our prayers if we keep on nursing resentment and hatred for one another."

After her country gained its independence, Tesfagiorgis set up a center for human rights and development. Speaking to a symposium on regional cooperation, she said, "Let us get rid of our enemies not by imprisoning or killing them, as many African régimes are known to do, not by belittling them or humiliating them, but by resolving the conflict."

Abeba Tesfagiorgis, Renée Pan, and Eliezer Cifuentes all have one thing in common: they say that it was the example of a Frenchwoman — Irène Laure, who after World War II found an answer to her hatred of the Germans — that gave them the courage to act as they did. It was Laure's story that Tesfagiorgis told the other prisoners in her cell: "Just as Irène Laure could not hope to see a united and peaceful Europe without Germany, we could not say we love our country and then refuse to understand and forgive our fellow Eritreans." A talk with Laure gave Pan the key to overcoming her hatred of the Khmer Rouge, the taking time for silence and meditation. It was the experience of seeing a film about Laure's life, *For the Love of Tomorrow,* that led Cifuentes to a new attitude. "What the Germans were for this French woman in the film, the military were for me," he says. "God has laid on my heart a task: the reconciliation of the military and the civilian population of my country."

We take it for granted that hatred can be passed down from generation to generation. The experience of this bold Frenchwoman suggests that love, too, in all its supposed softness, can have that same permanence. People who never met Madame Laure have taken her experience forward in unexpected ways. Peace dividends come in long after she has left the scene.

The idea that one day her actions would inspire not only these three people but thousands more around the world would have been far from Laure's mind during the nights in 1947 when, alone in her room, she wrestled with the question of whether she would give up her hatred for the sake of a new Europe.

Laure developed early in life the steel to resist wrongs and a social conscience that would not rest. She was born in Switzerland to a Swiss mother and an Italian father who had a construction company. Even as a child, she protested the way he treated his workers. Early on she identified with the Socialist Party. During World War I, she worked as a nurse in the south of France. After the war she married Victor Laure, a French sailor, and, like herself, a Marxist with no faith in God. They had five children and raised nine others as well. They tried as socialists to build bridges between countries and particularly friendships with the Germans, even taking German children into their home and working to save children caught up in the Spanish Civil War.

When France was taken over by the Germans in World War II, the Laure family threw in their lot with the Resistance. One son was tortured by the Gestapo. When Allied bombers flew overhead, Irene rejoiced at the destruction that would be wreaked on Germany. After the war she witnessed the opening of a mass grave containing the mutilated bodies of some of her comrades. She longed for the total destruction of Germany; she never thought that understanding was possible, and never sought it.

In 1946 Laure was elected to Parliament from Marseilles with a huge majority. It was the first time women had been able to vote or stand for Parliament. She became an executive member of the French Socialist Party. It was at this point that she was invited to a conference at the Caux center for reconciliation in Switzerland. She accepted, looking forward to a break from politics in Paris and to some good food for her children, who were suffering from wartime malnutrition. Despite her internationalist background, when she discovered that there were Germans at the conference, she wanted to leave. She hesitated when she was challenged with the question of how Europe could ever be rebuilt without Germany. Her immediate response was that anyone who made such a suggestion had no idea what she had lived through. Her second response was that perhaps there might be hope of doing something differently, though she still needed the spiritual experience that could break the steel band of hatred for Germans that encased her heart.

This was the moment she retired to her room. "I was there two days and nights without sleeping or eating with this terrible battle going on inside me. I had to face the fact that hatred, whatever the reasons for it, is always a factor that creates new wars."

On the third morning, Laure was ready to have a meal with a German woman. She hardly touched her food but poured out all she felt and all she had lived through. And then she said, "I'm telling you all this because I want to be free of this hate."

There was a silence, and then the German woman, Clarita von Trott, shared with the Frenchwoman her experiences from the war. Her husband, Adam, had been one of those at the heart of the July 20, 1944, plot to kill Hitler. It had failed and he had been executed, and she was left alone to bring up their two children. She told Laure, "We Germans did not resist enough, we did not resist early enough and on a scale that was big enough, and we brought on you and ourselves and the world endless agony and suffering. I want to say I am sorry."

After the meal, the two women and their interpreters sat quietly on the terrace overlooking Lake Geneva. Then Laure, the Marxist Socialist, told her new German friend that she believed that if they prayed, God would help them. She prayed first, asking to be freed of hatred so that a new future could be built. And then von Trott prayed, in French. Instinctively, Irène laid her hand on the knee of her former enemy. "In that moment," she said later, "the bridge across the Rhine was built and that bridge always held, never broke."

Irène Laure asked to be given the opportunity to speak to the conference. Many were aware of her background, but few knew what conclusion she had come to alone in her room or the effect that her conversation with Clarita von Trott had had on her attitude. "Everyone was fearful. They knew what I felt about the Germans. They didn't know I had accepted the challenge."

Speaking to the six hundred people in the hall, including the Germans, she told them honestly and, as she says, disastrously, all that she had felt. But then she went on, "I have so hated Germany that I wanted to see her erased from the map of Europe. But I have seen here that my hatred is wrong. I am sorry and I wish to ask the forgiveness of all the Germans present."

Following her words, a German woman stepped up from the hall and took her hand. To Laure it was such a feeling of liberation that it was like a great weight being lifted from her shoulders. "At that moment I knew that I was going to give the rest of my life to take this message of forgiveness and reconciliation to the world."

Rosemarie Haver, whose mother was the woman who took Madame Laure's outstretched hand, said to her more than thirty years later, "Your courage in bringing your hatred to God and asking us Germans for forgiveness was a deeply shattering experience. When I saw my mother go up to you, my whole world collapsed about me. I felt deeply ashamed at what Germans had done to you and your family. I slowly began to understand that these Germans who had also brought much suffering on my own family had acted in the name of Germany, which meant in my name also."

Irène Laure and her husband decided to go to Germany. For eleven weeks they criss-crossed the country, addressing two hundred meetings, including ten of the eleven state parliaments. To every audience she repeated her apology. With them went some of their compatriots who had lost families in the gas chambers, as well as men and women from other countries who only a short time before had been fighting against the Germans.

Seeing at first hand the suffering the Germans, and particularly the German women, had undergone and were continuing to face strengthened her conviction that a new way had to be found. She told a group of women clearing away rubble in Berlin, "I swear to you that I will give the rest of my life so that what you are going through will never again be possible in the world."

Laure's interpreter, Denise Wood, believes that she never turned back from her conviction to forgive the Germans and to ask for their forgiveness for her previous hatred of them. But the weeks in Germany tested again and again the strength of her resolve. Wood remembers Laure describing to her how on one occasion she suddenly saw out of her car window a road sign which read "Dachau." "She said to me, 'I thought I would go out of my mind ... the faces and the voices of many Resistance comrades assaulted me. I wondered whether I was betraying them by holding out the hand of forgiveness. At last a calm came over me, and I sensed a voice saying to me, "You are trying to do the right thing ... have no fear ... go on."'"

About going to Germany, Laure would say later:

> Can you think what it meant for me to go there? In my heart I had willed the ruins of World War II. I am a mother and a grandmother. I am a Socialist and all my life I have talked about fraternity, yet I had longed for a whole people to be destroyed. I had to ask forgiveness for my hatred from those people who were living in the ruins. I had to ask forgiveness from 50,000 women whom I saw, gray with fatigue, clearing the rubble in Berlin. I do not forget the ruins in my own, or other countries, that the Germans caused. Not at all. But the thing I had to do was to face my own hatred and the part it played in dividing Europe, and to ask forgiveness for it. Change in me brought forth change in many Germans. An idea strong enough to answer the hate I had, is strong enough to change the course of history.

As the Frenchwoman moved beyond hatred of the Germans, she also moved beyond class war in her thinking about employers, a hatred that had been nurtured early on by her father's treatment of his workers and reinforced by her training in Marxism. Her shift in outlook toward employers and people of wealth was so unmistakable that Guy Mollet, secretary of the French Socialist Party, threatened to court-martial her for her abandonment of the class struggle and her willingness to speak on the same platform with leaders of management. Léon Blum, former Socialist prime minister, sent word to Mollet that if he went ahead with his plan, he would personally get up from his sickbed to be her lawyer. "And if I do, it will kill me." Blum was desperately frail from his years in Auschwitz, and Mollet knew it. The court-martial proceedings were dropped.

"If I had continued as I was," Laure said later, "I should have spread hatred right throughout my family. My children would have started off hating the Germans, then the bosses, and who would have been next?"

Over the next forty years she and her husband, and sometimes their children, traveled all over the world to carry her answer of forgiveness. "It took a miracle to uproot the hatred in my heart," she said. "I barely believed in God, but he performed this miracle. I became free to struggle for the whole world, with a deep desire to heal the past. After I asked the Germans for forgiveness for having wished their country's complete destruction, I was finally able to work effectively for world peace."

Wood believes the dimension of Laure's experience of reconciliation was deeply rooted and a powerful hallmark of what she became. "I have always felt that the bridges she built and walked across were anchored in her faith in God, her wide international vision, her love of people, and her devotion to children which made her willing to pay a high price for their future."

Joseph Montville (see chapter 1) sees the experience of Laure as a model for relieving that sense of victimhood, and the violence associated with it, which usually defies traditional solutions. Although it is rare for national leaders to admit past national misdeeds, he believes that individual representatives like Laure can assume such responsibility. By their acts of forgiveness or contrition, they then become spokespersons for a new way of thinking and a new image for their respective nations. In *The Psychodynamics of International Relationships* Montville singles out the change in Irene Laure as "perhaps the signature event in terms of psychological breakthroughs in the Franco-German conflict" and "one of the most dramatic examples of the power of a simple appeal for forgiveness."

When Laure died, the *Times* of London headed her obituary, "Resistance heroine and healer of wounds."

Largely unnoticed by the world, perhaps because it is remote and small, the Pacific island nation of Fiji has been undergoing what is being called a minor political miracle. Elections under a new multiracial and democratic constitution, adopted by every single member of Parliament of each party and ethnic group, gave Fiji in May 1999 its first prime minister of Indian origin, Mahendra Chaudhary.

Two years earlier, Fiji had been readmitted to the British Commonwealth after a ten-year absence. "For twelve years Fiji has been trying to live down the shame of a military coup," reported the

Economist (May 22). "The result of its general election indicate that it now has the chance to make a new start."

In 1987 this coup, aimed at securing perpetual political domination by native Fijians, had overthrown the government of Dr. Timoci Bavadra, which drew its support largely from the Indian sector of Fiji's population. The coup, led by an indigenous Fijian officer, Lieutenant Colonel Sitiveni Rabuka, divided even more than before the two communities. Fiji's population now is made up of about 44 percent Indians who are descendants of indentured laborers brought there by the British rulers in the nineteenth century, and 51 percent indigenous Fijians. In the years after the coup, nearly 100,000 highly skilled people and business families emigrated; there were two devaluations, an economic downturn, and low overseas investor confidence.

In 1990 a new constitution was drawn up, but it was rejected by the Indian community, who felt that, besides being imposed on them, it was undemocratic and unfair in that it gave Fijians disproportionately more ethnically assigned seats in the legislature. In 1992, the coup leader reversed his position from being for Fijian political dominance to being a prime proponent of multiracialism, and a trust-building process was started. "We learned that we needed to re-establish trust and good relations between the communities and our political leaders on opposed sides of the fence," said Prime Minister Rabuka. In the 1999 elections he apologized to the Indians for his actions.

The 1997 Constitution Review produced a new constitution whose power-sharing provisions made it acceptable to the Indian community. For the first time in Fiji's history, one-third of the seats in Parliament were open to candidates of any race. "The objective of the new constitution is to make all our communities feel that they belong to Fiji, that their interests matter and that their contributions are valued." Rabuka described the new constitution as "a happy reconciliation of the different aspirations in a social contract to which we are bound for the long term." He said that in a multi-ethnic society, the solving of communal conflicts and the maintenance of peace and stability are preconditions for increasing the standard of living of the people.

History was also made in Fiji in 1997, when for the first time an Indian, Jai Ram Reddy, then leader of the parliamentary opposition, was invited to address the Great Council of Chiefs. Acknowledging his listeners as chiefs "not just of Fijians but of all the people of Fiji," he said, "We seek a country whose children of all races grow up with a deep understanding and respect for each other's cultures, languages and traditions." His people had been afraid of being "second-class citizens," and the Fijians feared being dispossessed of the land of their ancestors. "We had allowed fear to become our driving force — and there was fault on both sides. I think many of us who were involved see now that we were wrong. I reach out to you today then and I seek your blessings for a better way, a way without fear that has for so long cast its shadow over us."

Reddy said that by confronting fears honestly and openly, they had found comprehensive middle ground: "We have let light into the dark corners of the national soul — and found hope. We want to convert what has been a political culture of confrontation into a culture of cooperation."

One Fijian who did much to help Fiji to move from confrontation to cooperation is Ratu Meli Vesikula, who spent twenty-three years in the British Army. As a member of a family of hereditary chiefs, he felt, on returning to the country after his military service, that it was his duty to use his training for the benefit of the country, so he joined the provincial administration. When the 1987 coup took place, it was proclaimed "in the name of the indigenous people." Ratu Meli readily accepted this justification and was soon enlisted as a leader of the Taukei nationalist movement, whose slogan was "Fiji for the Fijians."

"I advocated violence, instigated violence, talked of sending Indians away from Fiji," he says. As a spokesman for the movement, he got a Fijian crowd to dig a big hole in the middle of Suva and start a fire over it, threatening to put Indians in this lovo (a Fijian oven in the ground). He became a cabinet minister in the interim government. When later removed from the post, he led a breakaway and even more extremist faction.

It took Ratu Meli five months to realize that the coup had not been mounted to benefit the indigenous people but to restore a certain group to power. For the chief, this realization came through a forty-day period of prayer and fasting, seeking divine guidance, which resulted in a "personal revolution":

> The change that took place within me involved the awakening of my spirit. I had come to realize that the "us" and "them" attitude I held was divisive and damaging. Once played upon by the use of race, it awakened prejudice within me and generated fear, hatred and greed. My group and I had become a powerfully divisive and damaging force in the land.

Ratu Meli began to look at his country differently. "I saw a Fiji that included everyone, a multiethnic nation free of prejudice, hate and division and encompassed in love. For the first time I found in the effort to bring our people together a purpose for my life."

He began to realize that God had no favorite race. "We are all his children, standing equal in his sight. I began listening to God and found new ideas were put into my heart."

After apologizing to a man he had treated unfairly a few years earlier and to his wife, Elizabeth, for years of unjust treatment, "the thought came to me as sharp as an arrow that I must apologize publicly to the Indian leaders and leaders of other races for the way I had treated them." This he did through the English-language and Hindi press. "They were victimized and made scapegoats," he says. His apologies resulted in his being persecuted, arrested, jailed, sued, and labeled a betrayer of his own people

New awareness about what had been happening in the country gripped him so tightly that he wanted to take on single-handedly those who had led the coup. But instead, he learned to forgive. "In forgiveness, everybody wins," he says. At a conference at the University of the South Pacific in Suva, he said, "I want to turn to my brothers and sisters from the Indian community. I would like to apologize for all the hasty words and actions I carried out three years ago. I ask you to forgive me for all those unkind words and unkind deeds I did."

Indians responded and took his hand. Y. P. Reddy, a respected leader of the South Indian community, said, "There is a great change. He is sincere. He and I and all of us can work together for the betterment of Fiji."

The chief welcomes what has happened in the intervening years and "a proper working of the rule of law." He points to the cessation of violence, the end of ethnic hatred, and a prolonged period of peaceful coexistence as an inspiring story. The will to put differences aside is, he says, alive in the hearts of his people: "When I think back to 1987-88, I shudder to think what terrible fate would have befallen my people had I not found a change of heart and been freed of fear, greed and hate."

One Indo-Fijian, Suresh Khatri, who has been working for reconciliation in the community, believes that within the next decade "we shall not only recoup economically but could make this a post-racism era." He senses that forgiveness is alive in the community, whether it is called that or not. At an election rally he attended in 1999, Rabuka asked any former Taukei to stand up. Some did. Next he asked all the Indians present to stand, then to sit down if they had forgiven the Taukei. All the Indians did so.

One cannot naturally assume from that one incident, Khatri says, that all Indians have forgiven what happened but "the forgiveness implied or inherent in the relationships of these leaders becomes specific through the example of Ratu Meli, his apology to Indians and to Fiji and Y. P. Reddy's acceptance of that apology."

One of the world's great cricketers is Sir Conrad Hunte from Barbados, who played forty-four times for the West Indies team and was their vice captain when they were world champions. He has the challenging belief that those who have suffered most have the most to give "in the task of humanising society," and he suggests that only through a willingness on the part of blacks to give in that dimension could some white people be helped to face up to their own need to be radically different. "In every broken relationship it is the injured party who must take the first step to rebuild the bridges," he says. In his autobiography *Playing to Win* he writes, "Hatred does more harm to the hater than the hated. For it makes a man ineffective in dealing with the causes of his hate. But hatred can be cured. I know, because it has happened to me."

After retiring from world-class cricket, Hunte devoted himself first to improving race relations in Britain and then to developing the youngsters in South Africa, particularly young blacks and women who traditionally have not been cricketers. From 1992 to 1999 he was the national development coach of the United Cricket Board of South Africa. The *Weekend Australian* commented, "Hunte, the consummate West Indian batsman of the 1950s and 1960s, is teaching his love of God, his love of humanity and his love of cricket to the boys and young men of the iniquitous townships in the tumultuous republic of South Africa." An article in the *Herald Sun,* also in Australia, says that through Hunte's involvement the program has been not merely a means of spotting cricket talent, but also a tool for promoting peace: "The two objectives are being achieved hand in hand, a thrilling victory for the power of sport."

The West Indian sportsman points to two forgiveness-related experiences in his life as keys to his commitment. The first, in 1964, was a foundation stone that freed him to take on his life's work; the second, in 1977, was a further building block. As befits the lay preacher that he is, he uses Christian and religious imagery.

In 1964, when the West Indies were world champions, Hunte expected to succeed to the captaincy after Frank Worrell retired. But he was passed over. He was stunned, felt an injustice had been done to him, and thought of quitting West Indian cricket. Garfield Sobers was appointed captain. But Hunte realized that he had often criticized compatriots who took their skills overseas if they didn't get the job they wanted at home. Would he live up to what he had talked about?

I knew I could not settle this issue, about which I felt so keenly, on my own. I needed a wisdom greater than mine. I asked God. His reply was clear and simple, "Stay on and serve the West Indies cricket team as number two." I accepted.

Then God spoke further: "Apologise to Sobers for your bitterness against him because he got the captaincy."

"Oh no, I won't," I replied. God did not argue.

For six weeks Hunte wrestled with his conscience, finally accepting the fact that however wrong he thought the selectors were, his bitterness was also wrong and would make him ineffective. He decided to apologize. and just before a series of matches against Australia he did so. At the end of the series, Sobers was presented with a trophy for winning, and Hunte with a trophy for "the player who has done most on and off the field to foster better relations between Australia and the West Indies."

In 1977 Hunte was traveling with a party in South Africa made up of fourteen people — he and another black, Sam Pono, and the rest whites. They arrived late one night in a small town with one hotel "for whites only." The leader of the party, a white, went in and was assured by a white receptionist that the interracial party could stay overnight. However, when they came in, two night receptionists, who were black, had come on duty and sadly told Hunte and Pono that they could not stay with the rest in the front but would have to stay in the back.

The cricketer was shocked but held back his emotion. As an international sportsman, he was used to five-star hotel accommodation. Pono, as a black South African, was resigned to such treatment. They trudged back to the servants' accommodation. As was their custom, they knelt by their beds to pray. Hunte thanked God for safety during the day and for shelter at night, such as it was. Then he could not hold back his tears. His body began to shake with rage. "God interrupted my tears. He said, 'Why are you crying? I promised you, did I not, that on this second visit to South Africa, I would teach you to know and understand the suffering servant of God?' My tears ceased."

Hunte thought of what he was experiencing. During the day he and his white companions were comrades in a common task of bringing healing. At night he and Pono had become "nonpersons," not worthy of care. The bathroom was closed, the toilet was filthy, there was no electric light. The walls were bare. The sheets and blankets were clean but torn. "That is the life of the poor everywhere. They face such shocks daily. They are forced to turn to God for healing, or away from him in despair. He was asking me to share the life of the poor. Where would I turn?"

Five friends who had died appeared to him in the room. He felt that they were there to help him bear the experience so that it became an ennobling and not an embittered one. Then he saw, he says, the privileged of every race, class, and color:

> There was a vast gulf between the poor and the privileged that no human agency could bridge. Only the outstretched arms of the crucified and risen Christ could bridge that gulf and God was asking me to stand with him in the breach and reach out to both sides. I was born poor and had achieved privilege. I was part of both. I faced the choice to turn to him, or turn aside to man's remedies. I forgave the members of the white government that had stripped me of my dignity and selfhood. I embraced the poor and privileged of every land.

Hunte says that although he knew he might face the ridicule and misunderstanding of friends, and the scorn of foes, he chose to be a reconciler, no longer instinctively taking the side of the poor against the rich, or the black against the white. "I became free to choose what was right in every situation."

He goes on:

> The doors to the future we all long for are barred and blocked by unhealed wounds of the past. In order for us all to go forward together as human beings there is a need for forgiveness of those who have suffered at the hands of the oppressor and there is a need for repentance of those of us who have caused the suffering. When forgiveness meets repentance, or the other way round, a new dynamic and creative synergy is released that the world has scarcely begun to tap. If we are ever to resolve our conflicts, personal, national and international, if we are ever to put right the wrongs that lead to war, we need to draw on that power.

11

Value-added transactions

"O Lord
Remember not only the men and women of good will,
But all those of ill will.
But do not remember all the suffering
They have inflicted upon us;
Remember the fruits we have bought
Thanks to this suffering —
Our comradeship, our loyalty, our humility,
Our courage, our generosity, the greatness of heart
Which has grown out of all this;
And when they come to judgment,
Let all the fruits we have borne
Be their forgiveness."

— Found in the Ravensbrück concentration camp, 1945

Ukonakala kwenya kukulunga kwenya. *(Out of the ruins good will come.)*

— Zulu saying

Forgiveness not only transforms suffering but also ennobles it. A hatred that is transformed into love, as the Dutch philosopher Spinoza pointed out, "can make that love stronger than if the hate had not existed." A reviewer in the *Irish Times,* writing about hostage Brian Keenan's book, *An Evil Cradling,* said, "From this horror has come something wonderful."

The point is not that one should court suffering and nourish hatred in order later to derive the benefits — like the man who banged his head against a wall because it felt so good when he stopped. But who can deny the hope given to the world when a person's suffering or hatred is turned to good effect, either through remorse and repentance or a courageous act of forgiving, or perhaps through a dramatic religious conversion? It encourages the belief that humankind can yet learn to do things differently.

A Vietnamese woman, Kim Phuc, now a Canadian citizen and a good will ambassador for UNESCO, is one example. In 1972 the Pulitzer prize was awarded for a photo of her as a young girl, fleeing naked and screaming from her village, which had just been napalm-bombed by Americans; it is constantly reprinted. Now, after a miracle of survival — including seventeen operations, a stint when she was paraded for Vietnamese propaganda purposes, a period of study in Moscow, and emigration to the West — she is set to become a missionary. The way she has overcome her painful past has, through articles and speeches, been a source of inspiration to millions. Her biography, *The Girl in the Picture: The Kim Phuc Story,* was published in 1999.

The Frenchwoman, Irène Laure, (described in chapter 10) became the instrument through which many people found a new effectiveness in life. Professor Henri Rieben of the University of Lausanne, in his book, *Des guerres européennes à l'union de l'Europe* ("From European Wars to the European Union"), writes, "Forgiveness washes away the hatred which grips her, prepares the way to friendship and leads Irène Laure to devote forty years of her life to a commitment which bears fruit in the resulting Franco-German reconciliation."

Some have found a way to triumph over setbacks and a freedom in expressing it that almost defies understanding — particularly those who have been hostages in the Middle East. Terry Waite writes in *Footfalls in Memory: Reflections from Solitude,* "My captivity was certainly a miserable experience which I would not wish to go through again. And yet, almost despite myself, something had come from it. I know that I was able to take the experience of captivity and turn it into something creative."

Simon Weston, the British soldier who suffered burns over 46 per cent of his body as the result of a bomb in the Falklands/Malvinas war, underwent seventy operations and will have to have more. He is badly disfigured, and can yet say, "It might sound crass but I feel that being burnt and injured has been positive for me. I've been allowed to do so much. I've achieved a level of contentment that I might not have achieved otherwise."

An author, a motivational speaker, a raiser of $30 million for charities, a vice president of two charities, happily married with three children, he is on a mission. Weston says, "I don't have time to worry about what people think of me — even if I am walking along like a wrinkled chip!" The most important thing if you become injured, he says, is how you cope. "If you spend your life full of recriminations and bitterness, then you've failed yourself, failed the surgeons and nurses and everyone else because you aren't giving anything back. Hatred can consume you and it's wasted emotion." According to an article in the London *Daily Mail,* "Wherever Simon goes, strangers come up to him and want to shake his hand. He cuts across all ages, creeds and social classes, and he seems to bring out the best in everyone."

Reginald Denny, the truck driver whose skull was crushed by a brick in April 1992, during the Los Angeles riots after four white police officers accused of beating black motorist Rodney King were acquitted, has a forgiving spirit toward the six attackers who stomped and bashed him with a brick and a hammer. A writer in *People* magazine says, "Even more remarkable than his physical recovery, however, is his lack of resentment toward his attackers." He is quoted, "I was the catch of the day. Forgiveness is there. It had to be. I don't have time to sweat those guys."

No one would want to underestimate the pain and physical and psychological damage done by incarceration, often in solitary confinement, or the wounds of personal tragedy or loss that never entirely heal. But thousands of lives, beyond the individuals involved, have often benefited and been blessed by their willingness to forgive.

The killing (described in chapter 3) of two English children — Johnathan Ball, three, and Tim Parry, twelve, in Warrington, as they were buying a Mother's Day present — and the wounding of 56 other people has now led to myriad initiatives by local citizens for reconciliation. Tim's father, Colin Parry, says that it was their singleminded determination to make their son's life and death count for something that has kept him and his wife, Wendy, going.

The Warrington Project was the first of a series of reconciliation initiatives, known collectively as Warrington Ireland Reconciliation Enterprise, or WIRE, set up shortly after the Bridge Street bombing by the IRA, with the assistance of the Parrys. The groups that form WIRE were established to help the people of the town to understand the situation in Ireland and to form a basis on which bridges of friendship and reconciliation might be built.

The Project was launched by the Prince of Wales and Irish President Mary Robinson, who also attended a memorial service for Johnathan and Tim in the local parish church. Enumerating the deaths and injuries caused by the violence over the years, she said, "Warrington has been drawn into its own best purposes by our own worst nightmares."

The Warrington Project is a long-term undertaking that seeks to promote mutual understanding by establishing joint projects with Ireland and Northern Ireland, involving young people in schools; training, especially of local government officers; and exchanges between religious, cultural, and sporting groups. "By these and other means," writes Canon Frayling, "the project aims to break down traditional prejudice and unhelpful stereotypes."

The Reverend Stephen Kingsnorth, a Methodist minister in Warrington, has visited Ireland frequently through activities associated with WIRE. Speaking at an ecumenical service in Dun Laoghaire, he said:

Just as Enniskillen plumbed depths, because of remembrance, a nurse and a grieving father, so Warrington featured Mother's Day, two innocents, and a dignified, visionary, parental response. Many of us are only too well aware of the need for repentance by all. When peace breaks out between Irish and British twinned towns, churches, communities, when reconciliation born of genuine penitence is forged, then perhaps present Northern communities will have a firmer rock on which to stand, and a friendlier community soup in which to share.

Because of the youth of the two bombing victims, the Warrington Project concentrates on working with young people. In Britain its program "Ireland in Schools," worked out with the Institute of Irish Studies, seeks to develop an informed interest in Ireland's culture. In Ireland it supports programs that create better understanding. In both countries it encourages student and teacher exchanges and in-service training. It has even introduced an Irish dimension into the primary school curriculum.

In the first days after the IRA bombing of Warrington Town Centre in March 1993, the Warrington Male Voice Choir, one of Britain's oldest and finest, assisted the victims of the tragedy and created links with groups in Ireland working for peace. Since then, they have given concerts for peace and reconciliation in Dublin, Drogheda, Belfast, and Derry. They were the first English group ever invited to participate, in 1996, in the St. Patrick's Day parade in Armagh. Terry Waite, who was born in the town, is their patron. In 1997, working with the Dublin Rotary Club and the Irish Peace Institute, the Choir was responsible for a "Christmas Concert of Peace" in Dublin's National Concert Hall. A 260-strong Youth Choir for Peace — children from North and South, Catholic and Protestant — was brought together, symbolizing hope and harmony. The Choir encourages cross-community activities involving the young people of divided West Belfast through a Warrington Fund established in 1994. In December 1998 the Choir arranged a Christmas tribute for Omagh, another city that had suffered a bombing tragedy. The program, with Terry Waite as master of ceremonies, was attended by victims of the Omagh bombing and by civic leaders from Omagh and Warrington.

On the second anniversary of the bombing, an Irish festival, or *fleadh,* now an annual event, was held in Warrington. It was launched by the archbishop of Dublin, along with the Warrington Male Voice Choir. It had the backing of the Parrys and the prime ministers of Britain and Ireland and was organized by The Bridge (named after Bridge Street), a project focusing on cultural exchanges — often with a community dimension, such as families hosting each other across the Irish Sea.

The Warrington Town Centre Clergy, made up of five denominations, has taken the lead in creating worship opportunities which explore the commemoration aspect of the event in terms of moving forward in understanding. The Reverend Stephen Kingsnorth writes, "One role we value as clergy in Warrington is to challenge those within and without the 'peace movement' to explore new ideas, to listen to those whose views we find alien. If reconciliation is to come, it is through mutual understanding, and Warrington as a 'victim' community, is in a unique position to listen, without being accused of collaboration. We can listen without being justly accused of being 'pro-Republican' or 'pro-Loyalist.'" He was invited to speak in Derry at the Bloody Sunday Rally in 1999. He said, "Warrington's gift was taking an isolated but shattering tragedy and a few deciding it would not make us the more firmly chained to our history. What happened in Bridge Street could form a bridge of learning to the histories of others."

Each year on the anniversary of the bombing there has been a "Community Peace Walk," sometimes in England, sometimes in Ireland. On the first walk, participants were greeted by two thousand people at St. Michael's Church in Dun Laoghaire in the Republic. In 1997, a "River of Life" pedestrian mall was opened with the release of doves by the mothers of the two boys who died. In 1999, Warrington Peace 93 was one of many Warrington groups and individuals helping to raise well over a million pounds to create a Tim Parry Johnathan Ball Young People's Center for peace and reconciliation programs, in association with

NSPCC child abuse prevention services and the Warrington Youth Club.

Summarizing what is happening in the town, Kingsnorth has written:

> The bomb had its victims: children buying a Mother's Day present, who lived in a town thought to be divorced from the 'Northern Ireland problem.' The event caught a mood, uniquely in the Republic of Ireland, which brought prime ministers and presidents to the town. Town Centre clergy were able to play their part, offering rites of passage, a civic role, a community voice. The Methodist contribution became prominent in that process. The media found Warrington useful, because it could articulate, because it was active, because it took risks, and a story was always there — the issue would not die so long as Anglo-Irish relations were an issue for Britain. The mood of reconciliation and bridge building was one most obviously rooted in Christian tradition.

The archbishop of Dublin, Donald Caird, said at a United Service in the town center that Warrington had become a byword for gracious response in the face of evil. Colin Parry makes the same point: "In Ireland Warrington is held up as an example of how a town can react with dignity following a tragedy." The deputy lord mayor of Belfast, Alisdair McDonnell, says, "It is a tremendous tribute to them that they have done so much for peace. They have turned hatred, despair and conflict into friendship, brotherhood and the hand of peace."

A Belgian teacher whose 23-year-old daughter, Ann, was murdered by her boyfriend has chosen to tread the path of forgiveness. Lou Reymen founded an organization of support for the families of victims and had a role in reforming the judicial process in his country.

When the news broke of Ann's death, Reymen immediately thought back to a meeting twenty years earlier with an Irish woman who wanted to meet the killers of her son and with a woman who had been victim of a serious road accident and was free of blame. "In a way these women had prepared me, " he says.

Within forty-eight hours, he and his wife, Mariette, were sure that they should reach out to the parents of the killer. "It was a question of putting our faith into practice," he says. To pray, to go to church, to preach, to open the Bible, that's easy, he believes. "But at that cruel moment I had to ask myself what I was going to do as a believer."

With his daughter not even buried and the young man already in prison, as he puts it, he sought the help of the local priest to tell the family that the Reymens were ready if they wanted to say something to them. Two hours later, the doorbell rang. It was the murderer's parents. The wives embraced, consoling each other. "How is it possible that we could set foot in your house?" said the visiting mother. The two couples prayed together for their children. Reymen says that taking this initiative "kept us from a feeling of hatred and wanting to take revenge."

Their initiative came about, he says, not through any virtue on their part but through a grace that kept them from a different response. "It is not in my character," he says. "Sometimes I have to fight against the spirit of revenge. If I am sick everybody tries to cure me. But if I am touched by the sickness of hatred, nobody bothers with my cure. On the contrary, everyone urges me on with, 'If I were in your shoes, I would kill him.'"

In an interview in the French magazine *Changer* (July/August 1994), Reymen described these experiences and his decision, as a result of sensing the need for it, to set up a support organization for bereaved parents. "Sometimes parents have a need to talk," he says, "but are often incapable of doing so." It started with four couples whose children had been murdered, meeting once a month over a simple meal. "It is around the meal table that one can talk about things more difficult to talk about elsewhere." Since then the association, called Parents of a Murdered Child, has been contacted by sixty couples, with half of them becoming members.

Reymen and his wife found that sharing their story helped others. A truck driver whose daughter had been killed said, after hearing what they had been through, "If these parents have had the courage to see the parents of the murderer of their daughter, then I do not have the right to kill the man who killed my daughter."

The Belgian teacher also decided to write a book that would contain not only stories but also help with practical questions about money and legal matters, and reference addresses. Published in French and Dutch, *Vivre avec une ombre* ("Living with a Shadow") was sent free, thanks to sponsors, to members of the parliamentary commission on justice, the minister of justice, his staff and the courts. Within a short time the book was being used in police training, with the president of the court recommending it to lawyers.

Reymen's hope was that his experience and the book could, as a professor of criminology at Louvain University said, serve to turn some of the judicial laws on their head. It is also, he says, a battle against hate in the world.

Repercussions of the work of their association and the distribution of the book have, indeed, included the appointment in each court of a social worker whose job is to get in touch with the families of murdered children and to be the go-between with the magistrates; the right of a family to have access to the inquiry files; the right to see the body of the child in a "decent state"; and some changes in the rules for national and municipal police forces in the cases of children's murders.

Before his daughter was stabbed to death, she had five times appealed to the police for protection against her abuser, but she always got the same answer: we can't do anything so long as nothing has happened. In fact, twelve hours before the murder her father had implored the king's prosecutor (an official similar to a district attorney) to intervene. Now, Reymen says, the police have made enormous progress in the field of prevention. They are also being trained how to speak to families. Six hours after the murder, two policemen had called at their door and been most insensitive in their remarks.

Reymen has been advised not to try to see the murderer, but he would like to speak to him. "Because that could help the people of former Yugoslavia, for example, to affirm that it is possible not only to forgive but to come together once again to serve the same goal."

He wrote in 1999, "Our life story is divided between 'Before Ann' and 'After Ann.' It happened nearly eleven years ago. It still is as if it happened yesterday. I do not weep as much as at the beginning, but the pain remains the same." Forgiveness is still for him the most difficult thing in his life, and in his faith. For years he could not pray, "Forgive us our trespasses as we forgive those who trespass against us." For some, he says, that is as easy as saying "Good morning," while for others it is almost inhuman. He had been told once that suffering strengthens in a person the sense of community and of compassion. Even to recall his experiences is still costly for him but "I can actually say I am grateful to have suffered."

An old lemon tree standing in the garden of a house in Ramle, a town east of Tel Aviv, in Israel, is a symbol of hurt and of healing. The house and garden were once the property of a family of Palestinians. During the Arab-Israeli war of 1948, the family was expelled. Treated as "abandoned property," the house was given to new Jewish immigrants. Today it is the site of the Open House project, providing educational services to the Arab community in Ramle and serving as a meeting center for Arabs and Jews.

Dalia Landau, who lives with her husband, Yehezkel, and son, Raphael, in Jerusalem, came to Israel from Bulgaria in 1948 as a baby. She and her parents were among the fifty thousand Bulgarian Jews who decided to immigrate to the new Jewish state. The family settled in a big stone house in Ramle that had belonged to an Arab family. She loved the house, its spacious rooms and huge windows and the lemon tree which almost collapsed each year under its fruit. "I grew up there without asking myself any questions about the past," she says.

One morning in 1967 after the Six-Day War, when Dalia was nineteen, a 26-year-old Palestinian, Bashir al-Khayri, turned up at the front door and said that the house belonged to his family. Dalia invited him in. It was the first time she had ever met a Palestinian, and the first time she had ever given thought to what had happened to the house's earlier owners.

She responded to his invitation to visit his family in Ramallah and enjoyed their hospitality. Their political views were far apart, each seeing events through the lens of the suffering of their own people. But there were the beginnings of a bridge. After the first visit by Bashir, Dalia felt that the home was no longer just her home, and that the tree which yielded so much fruit and gave so much delight lived in other people's hearts, too.

On a day that was unforgettable to Dalia, Bashir's father came to the house. He was old and blind. He touched the rugged stones of the house and then asked if the lemon tree was still in the backyard. He was led to the tree which he had planted many years before and caressed it silently, with tears rolling down his face. Many years later, after the father had died, the mother told Dalia that whenever he had felt troubled at night and could not sleep, he would pace up and down his Ramallah apartment holding in his hand the shriveled lemon that Dalia's father had given him on that visit.

It was painful for Dalia to get to know the unspoken history of her country. She had been led to believe, for instance, that the Arab population of Ramle had fled in cowardly fashion before the Israeli army in 1948; but in reality, as she discovered, they had been expelled. The story was convenient, she says, because it spared the invaders guilt and remorse. "I didn't stop loving my country because of that, but my love lost its innocence."

Bashir had been six when the family was forced from the house and ended up in Gaza. One day there he was playing with something which he thought was a toy and it exploded, blowing four fingers off one hand, an experience that was perhaps the trigger that set him off on a road of bitterness and revenge. In 1969 Bashir was imprisoned, charged with involvement in a bomb attack that killed several civilians. For fifteen years he sat in Israeli prisons. Passing the Ramle prison on her way to work, Dalia often wondered if he was inside but never had the courage to ask; it was too painful.

In 1985, when her father died, Dalia inherited the house in Ramle. She and Yehezkel decided to dedicate it "to some healing purpose." Wanting to do this in conjunction with Bashir, who had by then served his sentence, they sought him out. They offered to sell the house and give the money to the al-Khayri family. This was not to make a statement that all such properties should be returned to former owners but to acknowledge the suffering there had been. "I don't want money," said Bashir. "I would like to see the property turned into a kindergarten for Arab children so they can enjoy the childhood I could not have."

It was difficult to get agreement on how this should be worked out because of political considerations but, as Bashir's wife, Sheherazade, said, "For the house we shall always find a solution. The important thing is to keep the bridges open between our family and Dalia."

At the end of 1987 the *intifada* (uprising) began, and the Israeli authorities arrested some of the Palestinians they regarded as the most dangerous, among them Bashir, who was deported to southern Lebanon. On the eve of his deportation Dalia wrote "A letter to a deportee," which was published prominently in the *Jerusalem Post* (January 14, 1988). In it she chronicled movingly the ongoing saga of her meetings over the years with Bashir and called on him to use his new, higher profile to "demonstrate the kind of leadership that uses non-violent means of struggle for your rights, a leadership based on education for the recognition of your enemy and his relative justice."

She appealed to both Palestinians and Israelis to understand that the use of force would not fundamentally resolve the conflict. It was the kind of war no one could win: either both people would achieve liberation or neither would. She concluded her letter:

> Our childhood memories, yours and mine, are intertwined in a tragic way. If we can not find means to transform that tragedy into a shared blessing, our clinging to the past will destroy our future. We will then rob another generation of a joy-filled childhood and turn them into martyrs for an unholy cause. I pray that with your cooperation and God's help, our children will delight in the beauty and bounties of this holy land. *Allah ma'ak* — May God be with you.

This letter to a deportee was a courageous act. The letters that came in to Dalia were all supportive, and the paper received only one negative letter. One of her friends, though, would not speak to her for a while.

Bashir is a member of the militant Popular Front for the Liberation of Palestine and lived in Amman until 1996, when he was allowed to return to Ramle. He has published a book that contains the story of the house. Dalia criticizes his approach and is aware that he has never denied the terrorist act for which he was sentenced. But she respects his love for his country without respecting his actions. She finds him a person who feels the suffering of others and believes that a basic feeling of mutual respect has grown up and a shared feeling that one day a common destiny will be found.

In April 1991, responding to Bashir's earlier request, the Ramle house became Open House, a community center which houses the only nursery school in Ramle for Palestinian children taught in Arabic and is the first Jewish-Arab cultural center in the town. The first major program for both Arabs and Jews was a summer peace camp for forty youngsters, which has since grown to more than a hundred.

The Open House executive director is Michail Fanous, a Christian Arab raised in Ramle and the first Arab to sit on Ramle's city council. Yehezkel is administrative director responsible for financial management and fundraising. Support has been given from many overseas, including a grant from the World Council of Churches. George Carey, the archbishop of Canterbury, has endorsed the project and says that the story of the Landau and al-Khayri families and their friendship "symbolizes a new hope for the future." He was moved to learn about Muslims, Jews and Christians who had dedicated themselves to "practical peace-making." "The suffering of this region will not end," he wrote, "until the land is fairly shared; that requires an urgent political settlement. But peace also needs brave and imaginative ideas from individuals determined to create a new society."

Although the lemon tree has died, two of Bashir's sisters, Nuha and Chanom, joined the Landau family and Michail Fanous in planting an olive tree in the yard next to the house in January 1995, when the tree festivals in the Jewish and Muslim calendars converged. The sisters wrote in the Open House guest book, "Looking forward to a time when the fruits of love and peace will be enjoyed by the children of both peoples."

Another dramatic example of the value-added dimension of forgiveness is the response of the parents of Amy Biehl to her murder in South Africa in 1993. Nothing will ever take away the sadness of the parents at losing their daughter and the senseless ending of a productive life. But thousands of South Africans have been blessed by what forgiveness produced in that California family, eloquently summed up by the photograph of Peter and Linda Biehl embracing the parents of their daughter's murderers. As a Houston *Chronicle* article stated, they are trying "to turn the tragedy of her death into a celebration of her life."

The Cape Town-based Amy Biehl Foundation and its Project Mosaic is training women community workers and supporting violence reduction, mental health education, and other education programs, all areas that would have been dear to their daughter. They are using a USAID grant to train residents of a Cape Town suburb in baking bread.

Amy Biehl was on a Fulbright Scholarship in South Africa, attached to the University of Cape Town. She had gone there to support the black majority's struggle for freedom. She had earlier worked with the Washington, D.C.-based National Democratic Institute for International Affairs and had just applied for graduate study in political science, with emphasis on research on the participation of women in South Africa's transition. On August 25, 1993, the day before she was due to leave South Africa, she gave a lift home to some African friends and ran into a mob shouting anti-white slogans. Her friends tried to protect her, saying that she was a "comrade." But the mob saw only a white person, and she was stabbed to death — one of thousands killed in the violent political climate preceding the 1994 elections.

The news was telephoned to Peter and Linda Biehl. A *Los Angeles Times* reporter wrote, "The pain did not spin the Biehls towards rage, the way it often does. Instead a grace fluttered into their hearts that would humble even their daughter's killers."

Peter says that in many ways they had been prepared. Linda recalls fielding a constant stream of telephone calls and visitors and thinking of the words, "Father, forgive them, for they know not what they do." For years they had taken their children to Sunday school and taught classes in ethics. And while they had never been serious readers of the Bible, they feel few other words could be more appropriate, considering the circumstances of her death.

Amy had prepared them, repeatedly telling them that angry black youth were only doing what had been done to them by generations of white oppressors. They remembered her observation that when blacks died they were just numbers, but when whites were killed they got complete obituaries "with names, families, pets, everything."

"There was never any question about our position," Peter wrote in the California State University quarterly, *Reflections*. "It was a time for humility — a time for forgiveness."

The four young killers were brought to trial and sentenced to prison. Then they applied for amnesty under the terms set up by the Truth and Reconciliation Commission (see chapter 4). The Biehls wanted to participate in the Commission hearings. Amy believed strongly in the importance of democratic elections and had told them four years earlier that the Commission was a prenegotiated condition for the free elections. They announced beforehand that they would not oppose amnesty to the killers if it were granted. "We were certain Amy would concur." In a letter to the *Cape Times* two months before she died, she had written, "Racism has been a painful experience for blacks and whites and reconciliation may be equally painful. However, the most important vehicle is open and honest dialogue." The Biehls wanted to extend the hand of friendship in a society that had been polarized for decades. They wanted also to honor the support their daughter had given for Nelson Mandela's vision of a "rainbow nation," a vision of forgiveness and reconciliation.

The Biehls were besieged by the South African media, who plied them with questions like "Aren't you angry?" or "You mean you are prepared to forgive the killers?" This media response they found curious. "What should be so strange about this," asks Peter, "in a country where reconciliation and forgiving is national policy, rooted in centuries of African tradition?"

At the hearing Linda did not feel anger when the killers came in, only a sort of sadness, a void, a reaction which Peter says describes how he felt, too. They met the parents. "We wanted them to know that we understood a bit what they might be thinking and that if their sons should be fortunate enough to win amnesty we expected them to be accountable for their behavior. Accountability is an important part of forgiveness," he says.

One of the mothers was wearing an Amy Biehl Foundation T-shirt at the amnesty hearing for her son. Linda hugged her, a gesture which Archbishop Tutu said was a message that "sent electric shocks down your spine." A year later the son carved a model ship for Linda in the prison workshop. She told Tony Freemantle of the Houston *Chronicle* that she had no personal hate or animosity. So it was not as if she had to forgive them. "All I want is South Africa to get on with it. Amy died there because she wanted that country to go forward. Don't stop now."

Peter explains that to him, forgiveness is opening the door to a full and productive life. Forgiving is liberating. By contrast, hatred consumes energy, negative energy, and robs people of their productivity. Hatred, in the end, is a totally selfish behavior.

Peter Biehl ended his evidence to the hearings, after describing what Amy was doing in South Africa, with an offer to help in literacy training and education and job skill training. "We at the Amy Biehl Foundation are willing to do our part as catalysts. All anyone need do is ask." They have been taken up on their offer. They now spend half the year in South Africa, their lives linked permanently with the country.

Linda told an interviewer in Orange County's monthly *Woman,* "If you lose a child, you don't know what to do. It's a sort of feeling of despair and it's the end. But because of the letters we've gotten and the people we've met, we don't have to wallow in that despair. Amy has opened doors to us and allowed us to be involved in many ways where we wouldn't have chosen or felt comfortable before. When something like this happens, you don't have to deal with a lot of superficialities anymore, you have a purpose."

And Peter wrote in *Reflections,* "We grieve our loss, yet forgiveness has freed us. We can honor our daughter, we can remain true to her convictions, and we can carry on her work." They are often asked whether the amnesty process had brought them closure. He says, "We have never sought closure and have no desire to close the book on Amy."

It is not given to all of us to live through such testing experiences of violence and pain as have many of the men and women described in this book. But all of us in some degree or other share in the human experiences of hurt and disappointment and broken relationships. And all of us can experiment with forgiving or asking for forgiveness. The result can be rewarding.

Edward Peters, from Oxford, England, where he was working with a non-profit organization in the field of training young people, had been annoyed by something done to him by several friends and had responded in a way that hurt them. He decided to apologize and those friendships were restored. He says, "I felt as though a burden had been lifted off my shoulders. I rediscovered the inner freedom that comes from dealing with, and allowing the grace of God to shift, the blockages in my life."

Then he discovered that another friend had nursed a grievance against him for something he had done fifteen years earlier. "I was saddened by this and apologized. But it also reminded me how easy it is to carry baggage from the past, or simple matters like things we have put off doing. Wouldn't it be wonderful, I thought, to have a clean slate campaign to deal with all this baggage rather than carry it with us into the new millennium?"

Out of that new freedom and a simple thought came the Clean Slate Campaign, endorsed by a bipartisan national committee, and responded to by thousands. "If we all take at least one practical step," he told the public, "it would contribute to the new millennium in a different way." Each person who joined the campaign was asked to take at least one practical step during 1999 toward wiping his or her slate clean. Everyone was invited to respond according to their conscience, the only condition being that the focus was on what "I" and "we" can do, not on what "they" should do.

This is, indeed, the challenge of forgiveness — or repentance — for each one of us: to jettison the baggage. Not to weigh up the pros and cons, the expediency or otherwise, but to take time in quiet to see if there is any step, small or large, that we are meant to take, now.

We might always remember these cautionary words from Philip Yancey: "The only thing harder than forgiveness is the alternative.

On Turning

Now is the time for turning. The leaves are beginning to turn from green to red to orange. The birds are beginning to turn and are heading once more toward the south. The animals are beginning to turn to storing their food for the winter.

For leaves, birds and animals turning comes instinctively. But for us, turning does not come so easily.

It takes an act of will for us to make a turn. It means breaking old habits. It means admitting that we have been wrong, and this is never easy. It means losing face. It means starting all over again. And this is always painful. It means saying I am sorry. It means recognizing that we have the ability to change. These things are terribly hard to do.

But unless we turn, we will be trapped forever in yesterday's ways. Lord help us to turn- from callousness to sensitivity, from hostility to love, from pettiness to purpose, from envy to contentment, from carelessness to discipline, from fear to faith.

Turn us around, oh, Lord, and bring us back toward You. Revive our lives at the beginning. And turn us toward each other, Lord, for in isolation, there is no life.

— *Gates of Repentance,* a liturgy for Yom Kippur

Bibliography

Accattoli, Luigi. *When a Pope Asks Forgiveness*. Boston: Pauline Books and Media, 1998.

Aikman, David. *Great Souls*. Nashville: Word, 1998.

Anderson, Terry. "Out of Prison." *For a Change* 12.1:23.

Arnold, Johann Christoph. *Seventy Times Seven*. Farmington, PA: The Plough, 1997.

— —. *Seeking Peace*. Farmington, PA: The Plough, 1998.

Bonhoeffer, Dietrich. *Letters and Papers from Prison*. London: SCM, 1953.

Chong, Denise. *The Girl in the Picture*. New York: Viking Penguin, 1998.

Delany, Sarah, and A. Elizabeth Delany. *Having Our Say*. New York: Kodansha International, 1993.

Dowrick, Stephanie. *Forgiveness and Other Acts of Love*. New York: W.W. Norton, 1997.

Enright, Robert, and Joanna North, eds. *Exploring Forgiveness*. Madison, WI: University of Wisconsin Press.

Estes, Jack. *A Field of Innocence*. New York: Warner, 1990.

Evers-Williams, Myrlie. *Watch Me Fly*. Boston: Little, Brown, 1999.

Frayling, Nicholas. *Pardon and Peace*. London: SPCK, 1996.

Frost, Brian. *The Politics of Peace*. London: Darton, Longman and Todd, 1991.

— —. *Struggling to Forgive*. London: HarperCollins, 1998.

Gandhi, Rajmohan. *Eight Lives*. Albany, NY: SUNY, 1986.

Gates of Repentance. New York: Central Conference of American Rabbis, 1978.

Healey, Thomas S. *The Two Deaths of George Wallace*. Montomery, AL: Black Belt, 1996.

Henderson, Michael. *All Her Paths Are Peace*. Hartford, CT: Kumarian, 1994.

— —.*The Forgiveness Factor*. London and Salem, OR: Grosvenor, 1996.

Hunte, Conrad. *Playing to Win*. Bombay: Himmat, 1973.

Intergroup Relations in the United States. New York: NCCJ, 1999.

Ignatieff, Michael. *The Warrior's Honor*. New York: Metropolitan, 1997.

Jenco, Lawrence. *Bound to Forgive*. Notre Dame, IN: Ave Maria Press, 1995.

Johnston, Douglas, and Cynthia Sampson, eds. *Religion, the Missing Dimension of Statecraft*. New York: Oxford University Press, 1994.

Keenan, Brian. *An Evil Cradling*. New York: Viking, 1993.

Lester, John, and Pierre Spoerri. *Rediscovering Freedom*. London: Grosvenor, 1992.

Levin, Sis. *Beirut Diary*. Downers Grove, IL: InterVarsity, 1989.

Lomax, Eric. *The Railway Man: A POW's Searing Account of Brutality, and Forgiveness*. New York: W.W. Norton, 1995.

Mandela, Nelson. *Long Walk to Freedom*. Boston: Little, Brown, 1994.

Matkovic-Vlasic, Ljiljana. "A Cry from Croatia." *For a Change* 12.1: 23.

Minow, Martha. *Between Vengeance and Forgiveness*. Boston: Beacon, 1998.

Nussbaum, Barbara. *Making a Difference*. Florida Hills, South Africa: Vivlia, 1997.

Nunneley, John, ed. *Tales from the Burma Campaign*. Petersham, Surrey: BCFG, 1998.

Perkins, Spencer, and Chris Rice. *More Than Equals*. Downers Grove, IL: InterVarsity, 1993.

Piguet, Jacqueline. *For the Love of Tomorrow*. London: Grosvenor, 1986.

Reymen, Lou. *Vivre avec une ombre*. Anvers, Belgium: Éditions Standard, 1994.

Rieben, Henri. *Des guerres européennes à l'union de l'Europe*. Lausanne: Centre de Recherches Européennes, 1987.

Shriver, Donald W., Jr. *An Ethic for Enemies*. New York: Oxford University Press, 1995.

Smedes, Lewis B. The *Art of Forgiving*. New York: Ballantine, 1996.

Smith, Huston. *The World's Religions*. San Francisco: Harper, 1991.

Thwaites, Michael. *The Honey Man*. Canberra: Trendsetting, 1993.

Tucker, Margaret. *If Everyone Cared*. Melbourne: Grosvenor, 1983.

van der Post, Laurens. *Yet Being Someone Other*. New York: Morrow, 1983.

— —. *The Night of the New Moon*. New York, 1971.

Verwoerd, Wilhelm. *My Winds of Change*. Randburg, South Africa: Ravan, 1997.

Vrane, Andrija. Address, International Interreligious Seminar, House of Novi Nazaret, Banja Luka, Croatia, 1998.

Waite, Terry. *Footfalls in Memory*. New York: Doubleday, 1997.

Wells, Ronald A. *People behind the Peace*. Grand Rapids, MI: Eerdmans, 1999.

Woods, Donald. *Biko*. New York: Paddington, 1978.

Worthington, Everett L., Jr. *Dimensions of Forgiveness*. Radnor, PA: Templeton Foundation, 1998.

Yancey, Philip. *What's So Amazing About Grace*. Grand Rapids: Zondervan, 1997.

Index

About the author

Michael Henderson is an English journalist and broadcaster who has lived for twenty years in Portland, Oregon.

He has been president of Willamette Writers, of the English-Speaking Union and of the World Affairs Council of Oregon.

He has been host of TV and cable TV programs and has done more than a thousand commentaries on Oregon Public Broadcasting, for which he has been the recipient of many awards, including three George Washington Honor Medals from the Freedoms Foundation at Valley Forge.

He has worked in thirty countries and knows personally many of the people and situations described in *Forgiveness: Breaking the Chain of Hate*. He has been associated for many years with Moral Re-Armament (MRA), a worldwide movement for change and reconciliation.

He belongs to the Society of Professional Journalists and Britain's Chartered Institute of Journalists, of which he was for many years a member of the London District Committee.

This is his eighth book.

To order additional copies of

Forgiveness

Book: $14.95   Shipping/Handling: $3.50

Contact: **BookPartners, Inc.**
P.O. Box 922
Wilsonville, OR 97070

E-mail: bpbooks@teleport.com
Fax: 503-682-8684
Phone: 503-682-9821
Order: 1-800-895-7323

Visit our website at:
www.bookpartners.com